STATIONS

STORY & PAINTINGS BY

MICHAEL FLANAGAN

PANTHEON BOOKS   NEW YORK

Grateful acknowledgment is made to the following for permission to adapt their photographs for use as illustrations in this work: "Neptune" (p.23), adapted from a photograph by Robert F. Collins. ◆ "Index" (p.33), adapted from a photograph by John R. Stilgoe. ◆ "Chalybeate Springs" (p.39), adapted from a photograph by Charles Rotkin that appeared in the December 1972 issue of *Fortune* magazine. ◆ "Shenandoah" (p.47), adapted from a photograph by J.J. Young, Jr., taken at the Baltimore & Ohio Railroad's engine terminal at Benwood Junction, West Virginia. ◆ "Damascus Junction" (p.51), a modified image based upon the original photograph by Gary J. Benson. ◆ "Luray Run" (p.57), adapted from a photograph by James P. Gallagher. ◆ "Acomico" (p.73), adapted from a photograph by Van Jones Martin. ◆ "City Station" (p.97), adapted from a photograph by Steve Barry.

The original paintings were photographed for reproduction by Adam Reich.

Library of Congress Cataloging-in-Publication Data

Flanagan, Michael.
Stations : an imagined journey / story & paintings by Michael Flanagan.
p.   cm.
ISBN 0–679–43547–6
1. Man-woman relationships—Virginia—Fiction.   2. Railroad stations—Virginia—Fiction.   I. Title.
PS3556.L324S7   1994
813´.54—dc20   94–7596

BOOK DESIGN BY FEARN CUTLER

Manufactured in the United States of America
First Edition
2 4 6 8 9 7 5 3 1

IN MEMORY OF

WALTER H. FLANAGAN

1908–1984

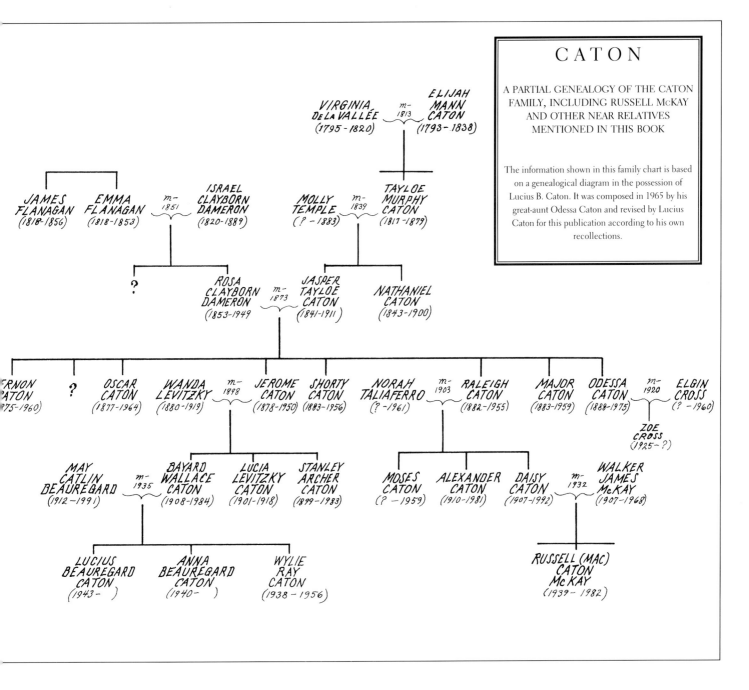

CATON

A PARTIAL GENEALOGY OF THE CATON FAMILY, INCLUDING RUSSELL McKAY AND OTHER NEAR RELATIVES MENTIONED IN THIS BOOK

The information shown in this family chart is based on a genealogical diagram in the possession of Lucius B. Caton. It was composed in 1965 by his great-aunt Odessa Caton and revised by Lucius Caton for this publication according to his own recollections.

VIRGINIA DE LA VALLÉE (1795-1820) m- 1813 ELIJAH MANN CATON (1793-1838)

JAMES FLANAGAN (1818-1856)
EMMA FLANAGAN (1818-1853)
m- 1851
ISRAEL CLAYBORN DAMERON (1820-1889)
MOLLY TEMPLE (?-1883) m- 1839 TAYLOE MURPHY CATON (1817-1879)

?
ROSA CLAYBORN DAMERON (1853-1949) m- 1873 JASPER TAYLOE CATON (1841-1911)
NATHANIEL CATON (1843-1900)

ERNON ATON 75-1960)
?
OSCAR CATON (1877-1964)
WANDA LEVITZKY (1880-1919) m- 1898 JEROME CATON (1878-1950)
SHORTY CATON (1883-1956)
NORAH TALIAFERRO (?-1961) m- 1903 RALEIGH CATON (1882-1955)
MAJOR CATON (1883-1959)
ODESSA CATON (1888-1975) m- 1920 ELGIN CROSS (?-1960)
ZOE CROSS (1925-?)

MAY CATLIN BEAUREGARD (1912-1991) m- 1935 BAYARD WALLACE CATON (1908-1984)
LUCIA LEVITZKY CATON (1901-1918)
STANLEY ARCHER CATON (1899-1983)
MOSES CATON (?-1959)
ALEXANDER CATON (1910-1981)
DAISY CATON (1907-1992) m- 1932 WALKER JAMES McKAY (1907-1968)

LUCIUS BEAUREGARD CATON (1943-)
ANNA BEAUREGARD CATON (1940-)
WYLIE RAY CATON (1938-1956)
RUSSELL (MAC) CATON McKAY (1939-1982)

The places we have known do not belong only to the world of space on which we map them for our own convenience. None of them was ever more than a thin slice, held between the contiguous impressions that composed our life at that time; the memory of a particular image is but regret for a particular moment; and houses, roads, avenues are as fugitive, alas, as the years.

—Marcel Proust, *Swann's Way*

TRACKS

Places are the only thing you can trust, my cousin Russell used to say. His words came back to me one cloudy day in late September of 1982 as I was driving south on a two-lane road, through a landscape of anthracite mines and reforested culm piles the size of mountains, where the streams had been rechanneled for flood control and the open hills were dotted with trailer homes that looked like they could be swept away overnight. What is so trustworthy about places? I wondered. Although my cousin was from Virginia, it was decided he should be buried in Minersville, Pennsylvania, next to his father and all the other McKays. After the service at the old cemetery, I got into the car with my wife and sister and we headed back to Virginia. Nobody spoke much on that long drive home through the coal fields. It was raining intermittently in the hills. Sunlight began to break through the clouds when we crossed into Maryland. We stopped for coffee in Baltic, at a luncheonette on a street near a railroad track, so close (the waitress said) people in their houses could spit on the freight trains rolling by. A nice touch. Russell would have liked that. After Baltic, we turned west on the old state road and continued for a few more miles past stone fences and weathered farmhouses whose yards were full of late-blooming shrubs. Here the sandy tar-jointed macadam pavement narrows and curves down to the base of the cliffs, where it runs along by the railroad tracks and the river. This was "Russell's way," a road lined with history markers, faded billboards, telephone poles and occasional abandoned wooden gas stations. By the time we crossed the river bridge, over the state line into Harpersburg, it was late afternoon. We were nearly home.

Russell McKay was passionate about railroads. The pictures in this book were taken by him. It was his idea to photograph the whole length of the Buffalo &

Shenandoah and the Powhatan lines,* to make a record of every "station," every wayside place the railroads had a name for. Russell worked at this project for six years or so, as weather and time and money would allow. He was always broke. By the early 1970s he had moved to Baltimore. So it was a matter of making excursions, a few weeks here, a few weeks there. Russell had the backing of a photography firm named Palmer & Hammond, whose studios had been located on Euclid Street in downtown Shenandoah for almost a century. Eventually a monograph of *Stations* did get printed, just as the old company was going out of business. I don't believe they managed to get quite as far as binding the pages. It seems the album disappeared from view almost immediately. I'm told that a few loose editions were acquired by some local libraries and historical societies. I tried but haven't been able to locate a single intact version, even in the collections that still list the book.

In any case, what we have *here* is one special copy of *Stations*, which for a long time was in the possession of my sister, Anna Beauregard Caton, and which has come into my hands now, along with Russell's logbooks, his working diary. I first saw the album with a rough binding around it that must have been Anna's creation. What a sight. The pages were gathered loosely between the decorated covers, and they were all yellowed and creased and torn. As far as I can tell, Anna is the only one responsible for these "alterations," the handwritten notes, and the weathering, I reckon, and even the rips and stains.

A few months ago I showed the album to Professor Jordan Stillwell, head of the Department of Landscape History at the University of Shenandoah. He did some local research and wrote up some introductory comments, which he has allowed me to use. Stillwell describes the album as "a tattered ruin of a book." Speaking of Anna's "intervention," he says: "The quotations we find copied onto these pages come from various found sources, books, journals, newspapers etc., as well as personal diaries and letters. They seem to have been matched to the indi-

---

*The thirty-mile-long Powhatan and the fifty-seven-mile-long Buffalo & Shenandoah are two separately owned railroads running mainly through Appotomac County, Virginia, extending into West Virginia and Maryland, respectively. The Powhatan, built in 1875, interchanges with the Buffalo & Shenandoah at Damascus Junction. The B & S, having begun operations in 1836, ranks among the oldest railroads in the United States.

vidual pictures by no guiding rule other than intuition. Nor is it clear by what system the color was later applied to McKay's monochrome gravures. What we can say, if only because it is visibly evident, is that the weathered pages have acquired a convincing presence of their own, as if a whole century's worth of deterioration had managed to be compressed into one decade by means of some arcane but carefully followed prescription."

◆　　◆　　◆

My name is Lucius Caton. I used to be a newspaperman. In 1970 I had a job in Baltimore writing for *The Sun*. My high school idol was H. L. Mencken. I was pretty good, but . . . well, things didn't quite work out. I married a city girl and we came back here to the valley and I started farming. We grow apples, mainly, and we manage a few dairy cows. Holsteins, Guernsey and Brown Swiss. It's full time. It keeps you busy. The nearest town is Index. Yes, "Look me up when you get to Index." This old brick house I live in has some history to it. Right now it could use a new roof. I wasn't reared in this place, but it was built by my grandfather's grandfather, Tayloe Murphy Caton, in 1840. There's a Confederate cannonball embedded in the south wall. I'm told they were trying to hit General Sheridan. Unfortunately, they missed. I grew up nearby, in Buffalo City. My sister and I have the same middle name: Beauregard, after my mother's side. Anna must favor it, since I gather that's the name she goes by now. I haven't seen her in quite a few years. She has a little house in what I would call the slum part of Shenandoah, our cousin Russell's hometown. It's not even twenty miles from here. She never writes. But this year she sent me a birthday card, handmade. *To Lucky* (that's my nickname), *Thinking of you.*

It's not easy to talk about my sister. But I should explain a few things. She's never been what you'd call forthcoming, that's for damn sure. Anna is an artist. These days, I don't know how she lives. I assume she's still painting. For a long time she used to work at the downtown branch of the Shenandoah Public Library. I think that's where she and Russell met as adults for the first time. He introduced himself as her long-lost second cousin. Russell was a carpenter's assistant at the time. He must have done some work on her place when she was living over in River City. That would have been around 1959. Anna was, oh, nineteen or twenty then. She was taking art courses at the university. I always said Anna had a little monkey face. She told me one of her lovers once said hers was the kind of crazy beauty "that got under your skin like a fatal disease." Maybe that was so. She was a torment to men. She was a torment to me. But with Russell, I gather, the score was about even. I don't know when it was Anna and Russell actually became lovers. Probably right away, knowing her. She always called him "Mac." No one else ever did, to my knowledge.

Russell's father, W. J. McKay, was a factory representative for the Gunther Piano Company in Shenandoah. I only met him once. Everyone said what a fine fellow he was. And storyteller. That I remember. They say W. J. was a great reader of the Bible. Religious in his way, without being too *Christian* about it. When Russell was a boy, he told Anna, W. J. would read to him every night in bed from the King James Version of the Old Testament, not skipping a single word until they had gotten through nearly the whole damn thing (excuse me) right up to, what is it? Zechariah, near the end, when either W. J. finally ran out of gas (he must have had a hard time with all the Hebrew names) or maybe Russell just grew up. Imagine, going to sleep with that Bible language in your ears night after night. Not to mention the *stories.* The plagues and punishments, the begetting and the wandering. Must have made quite an impression on a nine-year-old boy.

The way we are related is through the Catons. The Catons were one of "the illustrious three C's" of Appotomac County, along with the Catlins and the Clayborns. All these old families are related to each other. Intermarriage used to be the glue that held Virginia together. Our local art form. Now, the ladies at the Shenandoah Historical Society may have nothing better to do than get all worked up about genealogies, but believe me, the Catons were no aristocrats. W. J. McKay married Daisy Caton, Russell's mother, who is my father's first cousin. Daisy's father, Raleigh B. Caton, had lots of brothers. One of them was my grandfather, Jerome. Their only sister, Odessa (briefly married to a man named Cross), went to Smith College. She was a writer and local historian. She may have been the only sober one of the lot. Daisy's grandfather was Jasper Caton, our great-grandfather and Russell's as well. Jasper Caton was born in this house.

My father, Bayard W. Caton, was superintendent of a limestone quarry. His family had been in the business for three generations. They started with a farm, it was up along the Potomac near Engle, West Virginia. What they got in the end was a big hole in the ground. I mean big. I reckon we are a family of diggers. Dad had a few dozen men under him that he was responsible for, so he never got to go anywhere. Russell's father, on the other hand, was out of town on business a good deal of the time. I heard he would travel as far as Cleveland, Ohio. He always took the train. You never saw anyone so nuts about anything as Russell was about railroads. The family says he was like that even as a little kid. He knew everything about trains. You wouldn't want to get him going, or he'd talk your head off. The Shenandoah ran steam engines into the early 1960s, believe it or not, one of the few railroads in the country to stay with steam power that long. Anna told me when the B & S finally dieselized (that is the term) it broke Russell's heart. He would have been in his mid-twenties at the time. If the steam locomotive was a dominant image, as they say, in the American landscape, well, it was also a dominant image in Russell's life. Inner landscape, Anna called it. According to her, Russell started to have "enchanted dreams" about trains at the age of seven. He wrote them down at some point later. I remember seeing notebooks full of this stuff, with drawings, and intricate maps that he made, because he wasn't satisfied with the way the printed ones looked. Anna is fanatical in the same way, always changing things.

◆　　　◆　　　◆

What I now know about the railroads I probably learned from Russell. The Buffalo & Shenandoah takes its name from the two parallel rivers. Starting in Maryland at the B & O interchange at Baltic, the line runs west and south as far as Manassah, Virginia. It follows the Buffalo River for a while to where the river forks, and then it climbs upgrade along the Shenandoah. There's a short branch down to Corotoman, on the Buffalo River, then about eighteen miles further you come to the city of Shenandoah, where another branch goes up to Euphrates. That connects to the Pennsy (Pennsylvania Railroad) out of Hagerstown, Maryland. Also there's a crossing of the Norfolk & Western Railroad at Buffalo City I forgot to mention, not far from here. A lot of N & W coal goes this way. Down at the south end the B & S interchanges with the Southern Railroad at White Stone Junction.

The Powhatan line, which feeds into the B & S at Damascus Junction, was built and operated by the Powhatan Coal & Lumber Company to service a semi-anthracite mine they had in West Virginia just over the state line, but they did quite a business in passengers for a while, from the late 1880s until 1929, carrying tourists back and forth to the mineral baths and the spa, the big hotels in Camden Springs. In fact I believe the company even built its own hotel up there. The coal mine is pretty near shut down, but nowadays they're hauling hopper cars full of top-grade glass sand from a quarry near Chinaville. That keeps the railroad busy.

Now when Russell started working on that project, I remember how excited he was. He'd go out there on the B & S or the Powhatan, wandering along the tracks and, boy, you'd see him at the end of the day wide-eyed and covered with burrs, and he acted like someone who'd just been to paradise and back. A word I heard him use often was *spellbound.* He could get almost religious about some grubby place that most people would not even notice. He seemed to favor railroads that were "in a genteel state of decay." Here is one of Russell's diary descriptions of the B & S: "Graceful truss bridges, a network of rusty rails, faded lettering on the walls of old brick factories, signal towers, rural crossings, vine-covered telegraph poles, stone culverts, coal piles . . . the trackside milieu is a secret universe, preserved outside of time. Railroad space creates its own kind of *outlaw landscape* composed of fringe neighborhoods, flourishing along the unheeded routes where nature, never quite extinguished, comes creeping back into town."

Imagine Russell trying to explain that kind of thing to the vice president of the railroad. He had been at work on that project for a number of years, of course, and as Professor Stillwell points out, by the time it was finished, the B & S had passed into receivership. And Russell's only staunch supporter among the railroad managers was a fellow who up and died (see Luray Run, p. 56) while all this was going on. And so, my God, here comes Russell out of the darkroom and out of the woods (you had to know him, to picture this) after, what was it? six years of laborious effort. Maybe they've even forgotten about him, and one day he shows up, brimming over in that wild way of his, in the office of the court-appointed receivers, these bankers, mind you, and he presents them with his *magnum opus.* But what do they see? A beautifully illustrated tour of the railroads' most antiquated (and money-losing) features. No wonder *Stations* was "virtually ignored" (Stillwell), even by its sponsors, when the album was finally published.

◆　　　◆　　　◆

The way Russell used to carry on, it was enough to wear you out. I'll never forget one time he and Anna went to visit a fellow named Virgil Ross who lived up in Rainbow Gap. Ross was a famous train hobbyist; the basement of his house was taken up with an enormous model railroad that he'd spent most of his life working on. That *was* his life, it was all he did. Russell had several magazines with articles and pictures of Ross's layout. I swear, the photos were so convincing you couldn't tell the model views from the real thing; everything was built to perfect scale. Russell came back from that visit all wound up. He said Ross's scenery was equal to any nature diorama at the Smithsonian Museum. There was nothing halfway about Ross's obsession. That impressed Russell. It must have scared him too, the idea of taking his railroad dreams to the limit. A strange hobby . . . a paradise with no women in it. Russell would never give up *women* for model *trains*. But I could see there was a strong pull, a kind of enchantment there. Russell called it "little-boy world." Grown men got sucked into it. Virgil Ross, the model-railroad wizard . . . it didn't sound like he was all that comfortable in the land of the real. (But *realistic* is a very big word in the train hobby vocabulary.) The May 1973 issue of *Model Railroad Journal* carried a feature article by Ross; at times he sounds almost like Russell:

I think of my model railroad as a form of animated map, something like a sculptural picture, a God's-eye view of the terrain we are always traveling through but can never quite grasp. We construct a geographic facsimile in order to see what really can't be seen. Visitors tell me they enjoy discovering these miniaturized scenes even more than when they encounter the same scenes in real life. What we actually do in this hobby is manipulate and play with our own human scale, relative to a parallel small-scale world. There is magic in that.

Russell was always trying to "get to the bottom of things," but I don't think he had a clue as to where his railroad mania came from. Maybe he thought he'd learn more from an authentic nut like Virgil Ross. But Ross was too busy trying to realize his dreams. He had no time for introspection. Russell made these notes just after their visit:

The mini-environment of model railroads: cities, towns, countryside, reproducing those marginal places where the natural world meets the man-made world. Railroads, the connecting linkage in all this. Specialized corridors. Trains, confined to their rails, crawling across the landscape. They appear intermittently, unpredictably. Each passing is an event. V. R. builds a miniature stage, tries to duplicate these events. I asked why he was so fascinated with railroads. He said it had to do with "a circuitry in the landscape," the link between one space seen, another unseen, the thrill of coming and going, appearing and disappearing. Yes, I said, but what else? Why?

When Russell and Anna got back from Rainbow Gap, as I said, Russell couldn't stop talking about Virgil Ross and the model railroad and all, and you could see how the whole subject tormented him, but no one else was very interested. I remember we were over at Anna's apartment. My wife Suzanne was there too. She was always very good with Russell, she had a calming effect on him, although she hasn't always gotten on so well with my sister. Anyway, I remember we all went out for dinner. We took the streetcar downtown, it was still light out, and we went to Abbott Brothers, a little dive on Marypen Street that used to have great seafood. Russell knew some of the blue-collar locals who used to hang out there. I surely never heard him mention *trains* to any of those redneck pals of his. Not that night, or any other. I watched Russell up at the bar getting us drinks, and you could see how he loved it, how he loved to move between one world and another. Maybe that was partly why no one took him very seriously (least of all my sister) a few years later, when he started daydreaming out loud about going to work for some big railroad. By then I wasn't seeing much of him anyhow. We had our ins and outs, let's say. *Stations* was done, and Russell had gone to live in Baltimore. One day he surprised Anna with a phone call. She called and told me. Russell had signed on as a brakeman with the Baltimore & Ohio Railroad. He was in his late thirties. About two years later was when he got killed. It happened somewhere over in Maryland. I kept the newspaper clipping:

September 26, 1982. Indigo Creek, Maryland. A westbound Baltimore & Ohio freight train, traveling at an estimated 50 miles per hour, struck a

loaded coal truck at an unprotected grade crossing Sunday at dawn. The incident occurred on Dixie Road, near Baldwin's Farm. Witnesses say the driver of the stalled truck jumped from the cab and escaped with only minor injuries. The first two of five locomotives jumped the track and overturned, while seven loaded boxcars were also derailed. Killed in the collision was brakeman Russell C. McKay, 43, of Baltimore. Two trainmen were severely injured but are expected to live. The train apparently had obeyed signals and was traveling at the proper speed. The driver of the coal truck, whose name has not been released, tested positive for alcohol in the blood and was to be arraigned . . .
(The Baltic [Maryland] *Star*, September 27, 1982)

I thought Russell was wrong to go and take that job on the B & O. You had working-class men with families, who didn't have the advantages or the freedom that Russell had, these men really *needed* a good union job like that. I told him so at the time. He didn't much like what I had to say. After that, we sort of lost touch. To my mind *Stations* was the only real work Russell ever did where he was true to himself. He got to be good with the camera. It could have been a start anyway. It seemed to me, after that project was finished, that he just, oh, up and ran away from everything. As I mentioned, Russell moved to Baltimore while he was still working on *Stations*, but he kept making expeditions back to our area. Russell worked on his project for years. He always stopped for Anna, and she always went with him. I don't know why. It was something special between them.

◆　　◆　　◆

Anna. She was crazy about Russell. It wasn't that she knew or cared a damn thing about railroads. Why should she? Her subject was *Russell*. I think part of it was that she wanted to figure out what drove him so (he was a puzzle, for sure). Meanwhile she let herself be led through all kinds of forlorn landscapes, up and down those tracks, walking over rickety old trestles, visiting feed mills, abandoned coal yards, places where a woman wouldn't usually think to set foot on her own. That way, at least, she must have gotten to know Russell's world firsthand. Anna was never officially involved in his project, even though she did travel around with him, especially towards the end, where he spent a lot of time out in the wilds, photographing along the Powhatan line. I know they camped out once or twice up there. Sometimes she helped with the equipment. They were both keeping journals then. The last time he went away, Russell left his stuff with Anna. Notes, diaries, maps, everything. A lot of women in Anna's position might have made a bonfire out of Russell's precious papers. The way he kept going off, expecting her always to be there when he got back. In those days I used to drop in on my sister. It was always an adventure. You never knew what pet bird was going to land on your head, or where the furniture was going to be, she was always rearranging that apartment from top to bottom as if it was one of her art works. Anyhow, I'd stop in unannounced, because she didn't have a phone, and I'd say where's Russell? And she'd say, well, he had to go. And I'd say that's right: *Russell he's a ramblin' man, gotta ramble on down that line*. Actually I think Anna minded me being sarcastic and dumb more than she minded Russell being gone. In any case she saved every scrap he left behind. And if she hadn't . . . well, I wouldn't know today half of what I do about these pictures, or how they came to be.

The way Anna was with Russell, it did make me uncomfortable sometimes, I admit. Her history, for one thing: the whole business with Wylie, our older brother. Wylie gone. Not just rambling, but *gone*. It was quite a coincidence that Wylie as a kid was passionate about trains, same as Russell. I don't think those boys ever met more than once or twice as children. Wylie was one of a kind. Precocious. A genius, maybe. A born comic. Girls adored him, and so did Anna. She and Wylie had a thing. They were pretty tight. Wylie was as nuts about railroads as Russell. He was a science whiz, but he might have been a writer. I remember an essay he composed when he was sixteen. Not for school or anything, just for himself. Sort of a rhapsody about trains. Anna must have kept it (see *Luray Run*, handwritten note, p. 56).

Wylie was the star pitcher for our high school baseball team. In June of 1956 the Buffaloes won the all-county championship, in a 3 to 2 game against the Pharaohs, of Egypt, Virginia. They had a swimming party afterwards down at Patterson's quarry. The older boys always used to dive off those high cliffs. But when it came his turn, Wylie missed the deep water. He hit a submerged rock and broke his neck. I was too young for the party, but Anna was there. She saw it happen. My brother was eighteen when he died, I was thirteen, and Anna would have been just sixteen. It was a terrible thing for everyone, and I figure Anna never got over it. But she grew up, in her way. And then Russell came along.

I can't tell you about all that went on between them. Russell would always arrive unannounced; intense, skinny, boyish, dashing, obsessed. You could never pin him down. But then Anna was no bargain either. She didn't seem content to be Anna Caton from Buffalo City. She picked up a strange accent at school. People would often mistake her for a European, an error she did not hasten to correct. She had a vicious temper, the quiet kind that nobody knew about. Russell told her she laughed too much but that she had no sense of humor. That made her laugh. She became a little strange. I think it started then, in those days of Russell's coming and going. She began spending a lot of time alone. Not alone, really, because she lived with a menagerie. Anna made me appreciate chickens, which I've always hated. She did wonderful, funny paintings of her roosters and hens, all decorated with leaves and flowers and things. But she never exhibited them, as far as I can tell.

Unfortunately I can't say much about the technical aspect of Russell's work. Basically, the photographs were shot with Russell's 4 x 5 view camera in black and white. I did learn (from Anna) that Russell added a few train pictures that he had taken as a kid in the fifties, when they were still running steam engines. He may even have slipped in a couple of shots that weren't his own. It wouldn't surprise me, whatever he did. The publishers didn't seem to notice. God bless old Palmer & Hammond, they did a fine job with the gravure printing. How Russell ever managed to sweet-talk the railroads and the publishers into backing that project, so that he could do more or less exactly what he wanted, is more than I will ever fathom. But I'm glad that he did. Glad, anyway, that something has survived.

◆   ◆   ◆

I had heard there were a few examples of *Stations* still around, and I knew that my sister had at least one copy. I got a quick look at it once, at her house, about ten years ago. Already she had started to color the pictures and copy in some writings. I didn't think too much about it at the time. The library at some point had retrieved two unbound copies from the railroads' unwanted files, and so Anna may have managed to get her hands on those as well. One day I got a call from Joseph St. Clair, a newspaper friend of mine. We'd all three grown up together, we used to play in the alley behind our house in Buffalo City, and so Joey knew Anna from day one. He'd even been to see her recently, which was more than I had. Anna always trusted him. Joe told me more about the album. He thought it would be "a unique record" and that I should do everything in my power to show it to someone, or at least see it myself, before she did something regrettable. Joe said I was the only one who could talk her into it. He said he guessed, in a way, that maybe she wanted to be talked into it. That she was waiting. This old friend kept after me, month after month. And I kept pestering Anna. That is, I wrote letters. And I got other people to talk to her. Russell's family. You have to understand, I'm out in the barn with the animals by five every morning . . . free time is a luxury. I can't explain how it got to be like a mission with me, to rescue that book. Or maybe I do know why. I guess I had my reasons. That's just how it was. And she held me off, right up to the end.

It wasn't until April of 1992 that I had signs (another call from Joe St. Clair) that things might be stirring, that Anna might be ready to change her mind, that my recent calls to Russell's mother Daisy, now eighty-five and blind, may have convinced her to also write to Anna, and that it may have been Daisy herself in the end who prevailed. I walked out to the mailbox one morning and, don't you know, there was one of Anna's letters, in its homemade paper wrapper, with a drawing inside and a set of cryptic instructions. A treasure hunt? There was no postmark, no stamp on that envelope. She must have ridden all this way and slipped it into the box herself, before sunup. It came down to this: I would have to leave home one morning after milking and drive down the valley to Marveltown. I must go alone on a certain Saturday, to be there for a certain sale. I must look carefully for a certain box. If I didn't find that box first, then someone else might. There was a real risk, a chance of losing it. That was how Anna set it up.

I reckon Anna has had her reasons for not wanting to see me. Her plain eccentricity notwithstanding. It's true I used to put my sister up on a pedestal. She said it was my way of not understanding her. Anna: fragile as glass, stubborn as a mule. And so *willful.* But I went too far, that last time I yelled at her to stop hiding from life. It's not for me to judge, or be exasperated, or to say "she makes the wrong choices." Even if she is my sister, the exotic recluse, burning incense in her slum house by the tracks, sleeping on a pile of furs on the floor, and with her damn chickens and doves, her dogs, her parrot, her cat and her piano. Even if she does not, will not, own a telephone.

Marveltown, from Joshua Marvel, an early settler. It sounds like a name Anna might have invented. Well, she certainly chose it at any rate. It's a small town, about seventy-five miles west of Washington, D.C. Around there it's all farmland, with limestone outcroppings pushing up through the fields. The fact is, Russell spent a lot of time in Marveltown. He was always talking to Anna about it. Maybe that's why she wanted me to go there. I don't know. It's odd that Russell never used any of the photographs he took of the village itself. All we have is a picture of the road that leads to it. But he writes fondly of the town in his diary:

Started out at Nell's Village Restaurant. Scrapple and eggs with grits. Got an earful of gossip without half trying. For morning coffee Nell's is the spot. Went over to the barbershop. Spoke to Lyndon Fletcher, 73, who (I remembered!) cut my hair when I was 11 years old. We were visiting some Caton uncle that used to live near here. Loudon Street. Crossed the tracks, then the little bridge over the town run. Used to smell like a sewer. Cleaner now. I saw a fish. Down Loudon, one low building, I remember when it was a bowling alley. They still keep pool tables in back. Watched one potbellied old-timer playing nine-ball. Blue haze of cigar smoke. Watched him beat the hell out of some cocky teenagers. Stickley's Soda Fountain, Dameron's Hardware Store: the old boys still gossiping. What you may have missed at Nell's, you're sure to pick up at Dameron's. The same jokes, told better here, no women to be careful of. Smells good in these old stores. Must be the floors. How they've been oiling and sweeping and oiling and sweeping that wood forever.

There, I can just hear Russell's voice, I can feel him trying to *convey* this place. I can also hear him saying it's impossible: even when you have a picture to look at, you're no closer to the facts. Description is a slippery business. It's not what you think it's going to be. Russell says in the diary that the moment you start *telling* about something you make a story out of the experience. You can't help it, and it's already kind of a lie, and all men have this same urge to dig, to see, to collect. They go out and have an adventure, but that's not all. They need to report what they found. Someone *to tell it to*. Little boys use their moms for listeners. Grown men drag their stories home to girlfriends or wives. That was how Russell saw it . . . Hunting and gathering in the modern world.

There must be a lot of Marveltowns in this country. Now the people who live there, do they really need some artist coming in there to depict it for them? Look at the map, how the lines are connected to dots. And each dot with a name. Towns. Not shopping centers or planned housing developments or big cities. Actual towns. Most people still live in "rooted places," as Russell put it. That's what he was after. I have to hand it to him, he appreciated the difficulties. And it was his predicament too, *to describe is to destroy,* only much worse for him because he was doomed in his way to live it out, or not live it out, always trying to *depict* something impossible. He only just managed it that one time in his life, and that was by all outward measure a failure.

◆   ◆   ◆

I drove down to Marveltown on the appointed day. It was a warm Saturday morning, in May of 1992. The sun was out and the fruit trees were all in blossom. I parked in a shaded spot on Parthenia Street, across from the Athenaeum, where they were setting up for the book fair. The Athenaeum looks like a Greek temple. A history marker in front gives the building's date as 1853. It was used as a hospital for wounded Confederate soldiers before and after the battle of Easter Creek. Coming into town from the north, as I did, you can't miss the commemorative monuments placed at intervals along U.S. Route 11, the Valley Pike. The orchards and fields on either side of the road look so peaceful now, it's hard to imagine the fighting that went on all around here. It was very bloody. In 1864, as the marker states, "the entire valley was laid waste by Union troops." Yes, they burned our valley. They surely did. Now you see new housing projects here and there. And of course billboards and motels, on account of the interstate highway that slices right down through here. Even so, a lot of things haven't changed too much. I had coffee beforehand in town, there's a counter at Riddleburger's Drugstore, and they have postcards for sale, pictures of Marveltown from the 1930s and 40s. I swear, except for the cars, the streets don't look one bit different today.

They were just getting organized at the book sale. Cartons of stuff everywhere. I started talking to a woman who turned out to be Sophia Garland, the head curator of the Athenaeum. Very intelligent. They say she has a genius for getting people to donate money. Brown hair, beautiful green eyes. I guess looks can't hurt, in this line of work. Miss Garland explained how the book fair was an annual event that she had helped to organize a while back. The proceeds from this year's fair were earmarked for a fund to help repair and maintain the old building, which houses not only the library, as she informed me, but also "an irreplaceable treasure-trove of archival material pertaining to the Civil War in the Shenandoah Valley."

The day grew warmer as I began going through the books. The ladies had set up some long tables in the yard and along the library porch. There were all kinds of old books, and printed matter piled high everywhere. And bins and open crates too with loose folders, old fly-specked magazines and the like. Behind the tables Miss Garland sat on a folding chair with the library volunteers, answering questions. They had a cigar box for coins and bills. I suppose it's like archaeology, to go digging around through books and papers and other people's things. Flea markets are even more depressing. The shards of life. You handle these used objects and you realize there's no one to shelter them any more, objects that might have been sacred to somebody once.

Russell and the Old Testament. When I was hunting around there in front of the Athenaeum I tried to imagine Anna deciding to relinquish the book, which was *hers* by now. It was her baby. I thought of the story of Moses, how his mother set the infant out in a basket, wasn't it? to drift among the bulrushes, or the papyrus, hoping the princess would find him. Miss Garland (playing Pharaoh's daughter) helped me rescue the album. For it was she who found it, found the box that contained it, half hidden away under one of the tables. I'm not sure I would have succeeded alone. I paid Miss Garland twenty dollars. Lord, that smile of hers is something. You can't resist. You don't even want to. I dropped another big twenty in the cigar box. For the building fund. For Sophia. For History. I finally managed to gather myself, while there were still a few bills left in my wallet. I said good-bye to Miss Garland and walked back to where my truck was parked, back down the narrow brick path, in the shadows of the old trees, in the blossom-scented air, with the carton in my arms.

Before starting off, I could not resist a look at the prize. After all, I had "won," hadn't I? I laid the package on the seat. It took me about ten minutes to untie and unweave the colored strings that held it together. Of course it was no ordinary box, but one of Anna's ancient-looking creations. I should have guessed. The pages were inside, carefully laid at the bottom, wrapped in some kind of soft crinkled brown paper, under Russell's maps and drawings, and some notebooks of his. The hand-coloring had to be Anna's work. The condition of the pages was . . . well, it gave me a shock at first. I didn't expect the mostly loose pages, all torn and stained. Or the weathering. Did she leave everything outdoors, in the rain? with the chickens? Hardly a book at all any more. I don't know what you'd want to call it. Something else now.

STATIONS

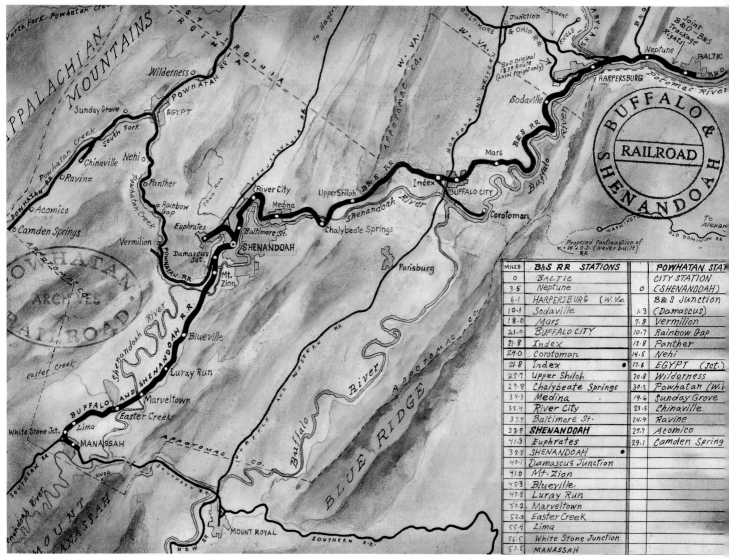

MILES	B&S RR STATIONS		POWHATAN STAT...
0	BALTIC		CITY STATION
3.5	Neptune	0	(SHENANDOAH)
6.1	HARPERSBURG (W.Va)		B&S Junction
10.1	Sodaville	1.3	(Damascus)
18.0	Mars	7.8	Vermilion
21.0	BUFFALO CITY	10.7	Rainbow Gap
21.8	Index	12.8	Panther
24.0	Corotoman	14.5	Nehi
21.8	Index •	17.6	EGYPT (Jct.)
28.7	Upper Shiloh	20.8	Wilderness
29.8	Chalybeate Springs	30.2	Powhatan (W.V...
34.3	Medina	19.6	Sunday Grove
35.4	River City	23.5	Chinaville
37.8	Baltimore St.	24.9	Ravine
38.8	SHENANDOAH	27.7	Acomico
41.3	Euphrates	29.1	Camden Spring
39.8	SHENANDOAH •		
40.1	Damascus Junction		
41.0	Mt. Zion		
45.3	Blueville		
47.8	Luray Run		
50.2	Marveltown		
52.0	Easter Creek		
55.4	Lima		
56.5	White Stone Junction		
57.5	MANASSAH		

Drawn by Russell McKay, 1965. Not to s...

THE BUFFALO
&
SHENANDOAH
RAILROAD

The concrete coaling station in Baltic is still standing but it probably hasn't been used for thirty years. Russell's notes describe the operations here in detail. I would not know about it otherwise. Originally the B & O serviced steam engines here. The terminal included what they call a back shop, with overhead cranes that could lift one of those monsters clear off its wheels. The B & S also sent their engines to the B & O shops at Baltic* for heavy repairs, whatever they couldn't handle at their own roundhouse in Shenandoah: boiler replacement, new firebox, or to reset the flues, that type of work. When the B & O switched to diesels, the B & S took over the coal and water facilities and they kept using that tower for another four years or so until, what was it? 1961, when they finally retired their own steam engines. I reckon it would take a ton of dynamite to knock that thing down. Railroads, you know, they tend to just let these things be.

Now I would never aim a camera at something like that, but I can see Russell's point. It depends on what you call beautiful. Water towers, roundhouses, viaducts, he said they were like ancient monuments, like the Sphinx or the Parthenon: "artifacts planted in the landscape, huge and enigmatic."

*Part of a complicated reciprocal arrangement, because although the B & O was a giant railroad compared to the Shenandoah, the latter nonetheless held title to the right-of-way here, having beaten the B & O's surveyors to this narrow, hotly contested stretch along the Potomac in 1832.

Baltic, 1 bȯlʹtik 2 balʹtic 1. Of or pertaining to the sea between
Germany, Russia and Sweden, called the Baltic Sea. 2. A town in
Temple County, Maryland, (pop. 12,243) formerly served by the
Appotomac Land, and presently (1) a division point on the Baltimore and Ohio Railroad, and (2) the
easternest station of the Buffalo and Shenandoah Railroad. Locomotives of both lines are serviced here.
(see Illus. p. 219)
— from Caton's Worldwide Dictionary of Place-Names, Baltimore, 1943. (The Parthenia State Library).

1. Baltic

My generation, born during World War II, witnessed what Russell called "the apotheosis of the Mechanical Age." We were there by the tracks when the last of the steam engines went pounding by on their way to Valhalla. The way those locomotives worked, you could see everything that was going on, all the machinery in motion . . . you didn't have to be a fanatic like Russell to appreciate that. Every kid in my neighborhood paid attention when a train came by. You stopped whatever game you were playing and looked in the direction of the tracks and you sort of stood at attention, for the whole grand show, the whistle blowing, those huge spoked wheels rolling so the ground shook under your feet, the smoke and vapor from the stack boiling up sky-high. After the train passed, you would go back to baseball, or Tarzan, or fighting the battle of Iwo Jima. No need to say anything. But then the changes came. That familiar deep-throated steam whistle was replaced by the sound of air horns. Now you'd run to the grade crossing to get a look at some shiny new diesel; that was a thrill for a while. You saw fewer and fewer steam engines, then one day there were none at all. It seemed, I don't know, *inconceivable* that you would never hear or feel them, never smell them, never see them again.

As late as 1958 a few of the Class 1 railroads, chiefly those owning or wit access to large eastern coal deposits, remain loyal to steam locomotion, enabling some dinosaurs to defy extinction. Here is a place to encounte survivors. An engine thunders throug Neptune, along its inexorable steel pathway, with a merchandise train bound for Cumberland and the west At this point the smaller Buffalo & Shenandoah has joint trackage right with the Baltimore & Ohio's main li through a lease agreement that dates back to 1840. On this 6.1-mile stretc along the Middle Potomac between Baltic and Harpersburg, the B & S shares briefly in the drama of big-tin commerce. B & O locomotive 6159 the "Santa Fe" type was built in 191 by Baldwin Locomotive Works, Philadelphia. At year's end she woul be found languishing with a few of h sisters in a scrap line at Toledo, Ohi fires stilled forever, a silent hulk, awa ing the executioner's cutting torch.

Lionel G. Marx. "Vanishing Species."
Railroad Monthly 15
(December 1958): 64–73.

NOTE: Neptune presents a puzzle. The picture appears to have been published as an illustration for a magazine article (see adjacent reference) from which the accompanying text was also excerpted. Did Russell McKay take this photograph himself, at some earlier date? Or rather, did McKay simply make the print for *Stations* from an unknown negative in his possession? The article by Lionel Marx gives no photo credits other than "Author's Collection." *Railroad Monthly* ceased publication in 1970.

As late as 1958 a few of the Class-One railroads, chiefly those owning or with access to large eastern coal deposits, remain loyal to steam locomotion, enabling some dinosaurs to defy extinction. Here a survivor is encountered. 2. Neptune

As it thunders through Neptune along its inexorable steel pathway with a merchandise train bound for Cumberland and the west. At this point the modern B. & S. enjoys mutual trackage rights with the Baltimore and Ohio's mainline, through a lease agreement that dates back to 1842. On this 6.1 mile stretch along the Middle Potomac between Baltic, Md. and Harpersburg, W. Va. the smaller line shares briefly in the high drama of heavy commerce. B & O engine no. 6159 (of the Santa Fe type) was built in 1914 by Baldwin Locomotive Works, Philadelphia. By year's end she will be seen languishing with a few of her sisters in a scrap line at Toledo, Ohio, a silent hulk, fires stilled forever, awaiting the executioner's cutting torch.

Bay, Chester Peake "Vanishing Species." Railroad Monthly XV (Dec. 1958): 64–73

NEPTUNE

The tunnel across from Harpersburg was enlarged and realigned in 1931. Quite a feat of engineering. About ten years ago I got a call from a Baltimore magazine. The editor wanted "eyewitness" stories, for an article they were doing about the tunnel. He asked if I had anything to tell, and I said yes I did. Well, that editor turned out to be an old flame of my sister's. Later it dawned on me, Anna must have given him my name. She still would have been adding quotes to the album. Maybe she asked him to call me, just to get my story in print. I wouldn't put it past her.

The Chesapeake & Ohio canal ran under the bridge here. Our great-grandfather Jasper used to ride down to Georgetown on the canal, with limestone from their quarry up at Caton's Landing, north of Harpersburg. They shipped the cut blocks down to Alexandria. Not too far from the bridge is an old lock house. The Park Service made a museum out of it years ago. One day when we were kids Dad brought us over here, Wylie, Anna and me. We parked by the canal bed, then climbed up the banks and walked out onto the bridge. NO TRESPASSING. We stood by the iron railing and looked down at the rapids. Anna held my hand. A passenger train came across while we were still out there on the bridge. Dad said hold tight to the rail. That train almost brushed us. We all got dusted in cinders. Then *voom*, into the tunnel. Gone.

After that we walked down the towpath to the Canal Museum. Inside they had an old register book on display. There was a space where the captain signed his boat in, with the cargo and weight, and the number of mules, to pass through the lock. The book was lying open in a case. All of a sudden Anna gets excited. "Daddy, look!" (She was about twelve then.) We gathered around, and right there in that open book was Jasper Caton, signed large for all to see. I was still spotty with cinders from the train and still shaky. I forgot about being scared. There was our name in a museum! I went around for weeks afterwards, puffed up with glory.

"Driving over the long bridge into Harpersburg, that was something. W the valley narrows, at the river juncti everything was compressed together, bridges, railroads, tunnels, canal, hor perched on the hillside, the town str lined with Civil War markers, which father always stopped to read, even though he must have known every o them by heart. Before the present br which at one time was paved for car traffic, there must have been, oh, ter others destroyed by floods or by the Confederates. The old road came up the mouth of the tunnel, then crosse the bridge with the B & S Railroad t which shared the pavement. It was a strange feeling to pass by so close to portal, the gaping darkness. Once we just pulled up when a steam freight came exploding out of the tunnel. T engine rolled by, big as a house, only few yards away, pouring out clouds o smoke. When we followed across, th bridge was still shaking. It was a hot The car windows were open. The air smelled like sulphur. This was 1953. was ten years old. Down below you could hear the rapids . . ."

"Eyewitnesses." Interviews with Traveler *Baltimore Journal of Industrial Archaeol* 12 (1984): 12.

"Driving over the long bridge into Harpersburg, that was so ... where the valley narrows, at the river junction, everything is confined, ingeniously fitted and meshed, bridges, railroad ... tunnels, canal, houses perched on embankments, the town street lined with Civil War markers, which my father always stopped to read, even though he must have known every one of them by heart. Before the present bridge, which at one time was paved for car traffic, there had been ten others, destroyed by floods or by the Confederates ..."

1931 · SHENANDOAH · 25

3. Harpersburg

The old state road came up to the mouth of the tunnel, then crossed the bridge along with the B. & S. railroad track, which shared the pavement. It was a strange feeling to pass by so close to the portal, that gaping darkness. Once, when we had just pulled up, a steam freight train came exploding out of the tunnel. The engine went churning by, only a few yards away, big as a house, pouring out clouds of smoke. When we finally turned and followed it across, the bridge was still shaking. I remember it was a hot day. The car windows were open and the air smelled like sulphur. That was 1953. I was ten years old. Down below ... could hear the rapids ..."

Baltimore Journal of Industrial Archaeology, Vol. XIII, 1984, P-12.
"Eyewitnesses" - Interviews with Travelers.

One Friday I took the day off and drove down from Baltimore. It was near the end of my stint at the paper, and I stayed the weekend at Anna's old apartment in River City. It was her thirtieth birthday. Russell had his own place, downtown in Shenandoah. It was the first of May, 1970. The day before that I was working at the paper when the news came in over the AP wire: *Nixon sending twenty thousand soldiers to invade Cambodia.* When I got to Anna's around noon, Russell was already there. They'd been listening to the news together. We decided we should do something to cheer ourselves up. We piled into the Jeep and drove up the Powhatan Valley, through Egypt, all the way to Camden Springs. Some relative of Russell's ran a place up there called Buddy's Lunch, where they made terrific milkshakes. There were some teenagers in the booth behind us, talking about how one of them . . . I forget exactly, it was somebody's mother, how she found this perfect Indian ax head right in their backyard, while she was gardening. Russell was avid about Indian stuff. He had a collection of artifacts, arrowheads mostly, that he'd found himself, just poking around. He claimed to have a "sixth sense" about where to find them. I didn't quite believe him. I could tell Anna was dubious too.

That afternoon, we were driving back to Shenandoah, coming along a little back road near where Powhatan Creek meets the river. It flattens out there, into farmland. All of a sudden Russell, he's been looking over at this field, and he says slow down, stop the car. I've got the *feeling,* he says. So I stop. Russell gets out of the Jeep. He walks maybe twenty paces straight into this plowed dirt field and he bends over and picks something up off the ground. He walks back to where we're parked and he holds out his hand and slowly opens it. And there it is, caked with red mud from the field, a little piece of milky white stone, about one inch long. A perfect arrowhead.

The first white settler here was the Moravian Johannes Soeder (1697-1750). Known for many years as Soed Crossing, the village was chartered at the same time the railroad was built. map of 1850 indicates a station stop a "Soederville." It is unclear how or wh the present spelling came into use. Records of the town, as well as severa early dwellings, were destroyed in 186 when Sheridan's men burned the cou house in retaliation for guerrilla raids Colonel Mosby's partisan rangers.

Roadside marker, Appotomac County.

This is a story about discovery. A you woman digs in the garden. She knee in dirt, alone in her backyard. It is 19 On the clothesline a sheet flutters in summer breeze like a flag asserting dominion over a measured, grassy wo The trowel probes through dry soil, turning up pebbles. Suddenly an astonishing object surfaces. There is mistaking its perfect pale shape. She rubs the arrowhead between her fing crumbling bits of clay from the finely scalloped edges to reveal a sparkle of quartz. For a brief moment the yard dissolves into an image of shadowy wilderness. A naked figure crouches the forest that has become a yard. His body is intricately decorated. A leathe hand grasps the stone point, then reli quishes it to the earth, to the darknes centuries. The woman is alone with fiction. She cradles the cool, obdurat stone in her palm as carefully as if it were a robin's egg.

M.F.

Discovery

The first white settlers here were the Moravian Johannes Forcke (1811–1850). Known for many years as Sodaville Crossing, the village was chartered at the same time the nation was built. Johannes Forcke, a minister, sold in 1850 and settled in Sodaville. It is uncertain how many others profited from the same sale. Receipts of the town's growth as several early dwellings were destroyed in 1864 when Sheridan's men burned the court house in retaliation for guerrilla raids conducted by Colonel J.S. Mosby and his partisan rangers.
— Randolph Marsh, Appatoman County

This is a story about discovery. A young woman digs in the garden. She kneels in dirt, alone in her back yard. It is 1973. On the clothes line a sheet flutters in the summer breeze like a flag asserting dominion over a measured grassy world. The trowel probes through dry soil, turning up pebbles. Suddenly an astonishing object surfaces. There is no mistaking its perfect, pale shape. She rubs the arrowhead between her fingers, crumbling bits of clay from the finely scalloped edges to reveal a sparkle of quartz. For a brief moment the yard dissolves into an image of shadowy wilderness. A naked figure crouches in the forest that has become a yard. His body is intricately decorated. A leathery hand grasps the stone point, then relinquishes it, to the earth, to the darkness of centuries. The woman is alone, with her fiction. She cradles the cool, obdurate stone in her palm, as carefully as if it were a robin's egg.

4. Sodaville

SODAVILLE

Was it some kind of family fate, the way Wylie got himself killed diving into a quarry? The three of us, Wylie, Anna and me, we would be the first generation of Catons since 1838 not to have someone carry on in the limestone business. We all heard the stories Dad used to tell: the rough work in the quarries when he was a boy, how dangerous it was. You had cave-ins. You had dynamite, where sometimes lightning would set it off. Quarrels among the men. Moonshine whiskey. Union troubles. In 1923 they ran power lines in there to operate the hoists to the crusher, and that brought a whole new set of dangers. Men, and sometimes horses, got electrocuted. (They used draft animals in the early days. Dad said the horses had their own time cards just like the men, printed up with their names and all, and they got paid by the hour.) Dad was missing half the middle finger on his left hand. He was one of the lucky ones. People lost eyes, hands, feet and their scalps down there in the stone-sizing plant.

Things were not the same in our family after Wylie's death. I think Anna grieved the most. She just went dark. For me, age thirteen, Wylie was already way up there with the gods. Then he just floated out of reach. There was a big funeral. I felt lost. Not only was Wylie gone, but something happened to Anna. A piece of my sister went down into that quarry with Wylie and *stayed* there.

Beneath the visible farmland is an underworld of Lower Silurian calcife rock permeated with caverns, grottos lost rivers. In many places the limest has been mined from above. By now older quarries have returned to natu along with the extensive works that c into being with them. Mars is one su place. Its only remaining building se as grocery, post office and freight sta Though the name is a family one, its planetary connotations seem approp to the mineral beauty of this site. Ma still survives on Geological Survey n and on the railroad timetable. Such names, as they outlive their usefulne become signifiers of a more poetic k They help maintain the poignant fic that "places" really do exist, within a constantly eroding landscape whose features are in reality as mutable as t ocean waves.

Jessie Hannah Scarlet.
"The Archaeology of Nomenclature."
The Buffalo River Journal 29
(March 5, 1984): 76–83.

5. Mars.

Beneath the visible farm... of Lower Silurian calciferous rock, permeated
with caverns, grottos, and i... ...laces the limestone has been mined from above. By now the older
quarrier have returned to a... ...the extensive works which came into being with them. Mars is
one such place. Its only rema... world... ...urves as grocery, post office and freight station. Though the
...name is a family one, its planet... ...ons seem appropriate to the mineral beauty of this site.
Mars still survives on Geographic Survey... ...railroad limestone. Such names, as they outlive their
usefulness become significant of a m... ...they help maintain the poignant fiction that "places" really
do exist within a constantly eroding land... whose... ...tures are in reality as mutable as the ocean waves.

Scarlet, Jessie Hannah, "The Archaeology of Nomen... ...uffalo River Journal 29 (March 5, 1984): 76-83.

M A R S

Russell had a friend by the name of Sylvester Peachman, who was part Shawnee Indian. He was a tower operator for the N & W, at the interlocking* where the Valley Line crosses the B & S in Buffalo City. Our house wasn't but a few blocks from there. A few years ago they installed unmanned signals at the crossing, and that old wooden tower is boarded up now.

Russell got this story from Peachman: In the summer of 1957 there was another photographer who came along this way taking pictures of the N & W, mostly at night. He'd be out there with his flash cameras in the dark, prowling around the tracks at all kinds of hours. His name was Luther Lincoln. He was on good terms with the N & W dispatchers and some of the tower men, and so he knew Peachman. This fellow Lincoln even had a special key to the phone boxes along the line. Now the railroad had (and still has) strict rules. You sure as hell better not have any unauthorized visitors up there in that tower with you. Especially not at night. Especially not a woman at night. But Peachman did one time. He's got this woman up there, and they're fooling around, and all of a sudden *the telephone rings.* It's about 2:00 A.M., and he's just let a big N & W coal train pass through there. There shouldn't be another train for four more hours, until the B & S runs its morning local. But that's not due by until 6:00 A.M. So the only thing Peachman can think of is *My wife!* Well, he drops the girl and picks up the phone. He hears a man's voice on the other end, very rough. "Peachman, this is Detective Donahue, Railroad Police. We're sending a man over right now to relieve you!" Now he's really shaking. There's no place to hide the woman, and already he hears footsteps, it sounds like *two* men, coming up the outside steps. The door opens. Flashbulbs go off. And there stands Luther Lincoln, with a big camera slung around his neck, like one of those tabloid photo guys, with his assistant, the two of them laughing fit to be tied. Lucky Peachman had a sense of humor too. He took it all right. I asked Russell what about the girl. Well, I guess she calmed down. And Peachman, his wife divorced him awhile later and he married that tower girl.

*Where the tracks of two railroads cross each other at grade level, the "crossing diamond" may be protected by a system of interlocking signals controlled (less frequently today) from a manned tower. The signals themselves usually consist of lights centered in a circular black target, mounted in a vertical row on a mast so as to be visible to the engineers of oncoming trains. The physical arrangement of the entire track-signaled area is known as an interlocking plant.

The name Beau Fleuve was given to t place by Sophie Clayborn, the French wife of Temple Clayborn, who established a plantation here in 1750 on a point of land near the confluence of the north and south branches of the Shenandoah River. The latter came to be known as the Buffalo. A town of th name grew to become the present city Little remains of the original estate except for some brick outbuildings tha escaped the Federal bombardment of 1864. Presently the Norfolk & Wester Railway's Valley Line passes through portion of the old farm, still owned by descendants of the Clayborn family.

Road sign, state historical marker no. A-25.

BUFFALO CITY

<big>H</big>ow this place got its name, I wish I knew. Index is where the branch line forks off to Corotoman, and there used to be a little wooden station here. It burned down one Halloween night about ten years ago. There are only a few buildings left besides the feed mill. They closed the post office in 1978. You won't find Index on your standard road map. Probably the Indians would have had a name for this spot where the creek comes down over the rocks and widens out. The B & S ran its first train through here in 1836. By then the Indians were gone. This track is almost ancient, as America goes, like the Roman roads in England. Nowadays the railroad evokes nostalgia. Russell was wary of that word. He was bothered when people took it to mean bittersweet or sentimental. That was not Russell's view of the past. I can still hear him say *bitter, yes! sweet, no!*

It has been nearly ten years now since Anna was inside my house. Our farm here is only about three miles from the tracks. Anna told me that once she and Russell had a terrible fight, right at this crossing, when he was working on *Stations.* (The old cast-iron sign is still there, by the way. STOP LOOK AND LISTEN.) Russell took a picture of the crossing as a coal train was going through. They had words, and Anna grabbed the camera and she went and threw it in the creek. Russell came back later alone and did the shot over. No train. Anna said she helped Russell make a better picture. More poetic, she said, to leave out the train.

crossing 1. The place where something, as a roadway or waterway, may crossed; as, at a street *crossing.* 2. In railroads: (1) a place where two roads intersect on the same level, particular when one of them is a railway, often guarded by a St. Andrew's cross (the c *decussata* or oblique cross, common i ancient sculpture)—cf. **cross**: a sacred or mystical symbol in many ancient religions, supposed to have been originally emblematic of the union of the active and passive elements in nature. **grade crossing**‡.

cross'ing, 1 kras'ŋ) cross'ing, n 2 the place where something _____ roadway or waterway may be crossed; as at a street crossing. 3. In railroad: (2) _____ ce where two roads intersect on the same level _____ ticularly, where one of them is a railwa_____, grade crossing, a place often guarded by a _____ Anthony cross* (the crux decussata or _____ ligne cross, common in ancient sculpture) _____ cross _____ cross _____, a sacred or mystical symbol in many ancient religions, supposed to have been originally emblematic of the union of active and passive elements in nature....

*On trouve la un passage à niveaux, ainsi que le Saint-André portant l'inscription "traversée de voie ferrée".

7 Index

The author of this quote that Anna found, his name was Lightfoot Early.* He and my father knew each other as kids. His home place was down by the river and it was said to be full of old bricks and bottles lined up on shelves and all kinds of artifacts he managed to "salvage" from the Catlin ruins.

Lightfoot was descended from General Jubal Early of the Confederate Army. About four years ago Mr. Early shot himself in the head with a revolver. It was in all the papers. He had no family. He was an old man, he lived alone and he had TB. He left a note saying he didn't want to be a burden on anybody.

Mr. Early happened to live close by what used to be the camp meeting grounds at Corotoman. Of course it was *all* Catlin plantation land before that. As kids we used to hike down there. The tabernacle was in a big clearing near the river. They kept the undergrowth cleared out and the grass cut, and the earth was stamped down around it. The building was whitewashed wood, open all around, on columns, under a big spreading roof that had a cupola on top. Folks used to come from all over to sing hymns and carry on, back in the revival days. No insect repellent then. People wore lots of clothes in the 1890s, maybe the mosquitoes didn't get to them. But the heat must have been murder. The camp meetings ended in 1929, and it was twenty-five years later that I used to go and play around there. I remember how that brick floor smelled, damp and mossy, it was open all year round to the elements. Some farmer owned it, he tried to keep the place up for a while, as a kind of recreation center, although it was already half gone then, on account of a tree falling on part of it. But in the fifties I remember they had a Coca-Cola machine in there and a couple of Ping-Pong tables, and broken chairs and spindle-back benches piled up in one corner, and an upright piano with an outboard motor leaning up against it, and some fishnets and oars, and yellow wooden cartons of empty pop bottles, and big lazy blue wasps in the rafters.

"They used to hold camp meetings down in Corotoman, under the trees. Then the Baptists, I think it was, built tabernacle, a big wooden roof open or the sides, with a belfry. That's where n grandparents met. The B & S already had a branch line there. It left the ma at Index, crossed over the N & W just south of Buffalo City, coming down th north bank of the river on a steep grad Around 1910 the railroad sponsored a hotel for the camp meeting crowd. No body cared much for local history then the foundations of the Catlin house w covered in poison ivy when I dug arou there in 1935. We found a two-hundre year-old wine bottle with the lead sea still intact. Everything fell into the cel you see, on account of the fire. There were hinges and locks too. Bits of blue and white china. Beautiful things. No it looks like the Amazon jungle back i there. Gardiner Catlin built the house in 1720. He sent home to England for the hardware and carved stone. He wa known as 'King' Catlin because his la covered the whole northern valley, tw counties. People don't know this place The passenger local was discontinued 1942. There's still a freight train twice week to service the quarry and the fac tory. That's all I know."

"Eyewitnesses." River People Remember. *Baltimore Journal of Industrial Archaeolog* (1985): 23.

*Lightfoot B. Early managed the Buffalo River Furniture Factory for nearly forty years, until his retirement in 1975. The firm, which was founded in 1890 by his father, William Early, employed about fifty skilled craftsmen. In describing the Catlin mansion Early had incorrectly given its date as 1720. Actually, the main Catlin house was not constructed until 1790.

APPOTC
COU

M·F·

S. Corotoman

People don't know this place. The passenger local was discontinued in 1942. There is still a freight train, twice a week, to service the quarry and the factory. That's all of it now.

"Equicinnoble." River People Remember. Baltimore Journal of Industrial Archeology. Vol. XIII (1985) p. 23.

"They used to hold camp meeting down in Corotoman, under the trees. Then the Baptists, I think it was, built a tabernacle, a big wooden roof open on the sides, with a belfry. That's where my grandparents met. The B. & J. already had a branch line there. It left the main at Index, crossed over the N. & W. just south of Buffalo City, coming down the north bank of the river on a steep grade. Around 1910 the railroad sponsored a hotel for the camp-meeting crowd.... Nobody cared much for local history then. The foundations of the Catlin house were covered in poison ivy when I dug around there in 1935. We found a hundred year old wine bottle with the lead seal still intact. Everything fell into the cellar, you see, on account of the fire. Fine wrought hinges and locks too. Bits of blue and white china. Beautiful things. Now it looks like Amazon jungle back in there. Gardiner Catlin built the house in 1720. He sent home to England for the hardware and carved stone. He was known as "King" because his land covered the whole northern valley, two counties.

COROTOMAN

Anna didn't really start painting until she left home. Before that she played the piano. She had a gift for it. There was a famous European teacher over at the university, his name was Ignatz Mauser,* and Anna started studying piano with him when she was twelve. I don't know how Mauser ever landed in Shenandoah, or why he wanted to live in a little place like Upper Shiloh. But that's where his apartment was, and that's where Anna used to go for her lessons every week. Momma kept a Steinway baby grand in the parlor. When Anna was almost sixteen she was playing Mozart and Beethoven sonatas. I cared more then about baseball, but even so, I'd lie on the rug with my eyes closed sometimes and listen to her play. One of those Mozart pieces, it had a long slow section, and I'd start to feel chills go through me and then the music would sort of *explode* like a volcano, when she got to a certain part. After Wylie died, Anna pretty much stopped playing. Mr. Mauser even came to our house to speak to my parents about her. But what could they do?

What gets me is Anna could have lived, I don't know, anywhere. Why stay in Shenandoah? Mauser told her once she *practiced* better than any student he ever had. But that was just it, it seemed like she was always practicing. I mean even later. Always waiting for something, I don't know know what. After Russell's accident Anna left River City and got her own little house in Shenandoah. I went down there one afternoon. She made tea. It started out friendly, but then I got brave and said what was really on my mind. I said it was time to let go of the dead. I said no man was ever going to save her anyway, so why hold on to ghosts, she ought to be in the world more, maybe move to New York, not be such a recluse, and so on. And I said she was too damn secretive, always keeping me at arm's length. I guess it's obvious I felt resentful. Lost my temper. She went silent on me. I can't say as I blame her now, the way I acted. I've had a few years to think about that. It wasn't until later that it began to dawn on me, maybe Anna knows a lot more about some things than I do.

Early evening . . . the Upper Shiloh Hotel, on the town's only through stre[et]. Their upstairs room at the rear overlo[oks] a jungle of sumac and honeysuckle th[at] slopes down to the railroad track. A freight train rumbles slowly along the riverside embankment and disappears through a blackened portal, into a sto[ne] tunnel beneath the old buildings on River Street, making the chinaware ra[ttle] in kitchen cupboards. While downstairs at the Powhatan Bar, tumblers a[nd] whiskey bottles vibrate in packed rows unheard above laughter and jukebox music and the clatter of billiard balls, floating upward on the heavy summe[r] air, to merge with train sounds and th[e] night song of insects. Even the bed trembles in this room. She wonders aloud at his need to be here. He can't explain these railroad dreams. Tomor[row] they will drive on to Shenandoah, to [the] City Library. It's time to lay bare the etymology of nostalgia.

*Ignatz Mauser (1900–1989) studied in Germany with the great Artur Schnabel.

Early evening in _____, from a rear window in the Upper Shiloh Hotel on the town's only ___ th street ___ looks ___ in a steep sloping jungle of sumac and honeysuckle to the railroad tracks below. A slow freight train _____ then through the blackened limestone tunnel beneath the nineteenth century, _____ River Street _____ passage with a tinkling of chinaware in kitchen cupboards. Downstairs rows of glasses and whiskey bottles _____ unnoticed on their shelves at the Powhatan Bar — no match for jukebox music, laughter and the clatter of ___ Bar sounds float upstairs on heavy summer air all merging _____ humble of boxcars and the night song of ___

M F

_____ questioning ... Why ___ the ___, the maps, the ___ , she ___ ___ they'll drive on to Shenandoah ___ library will have ___ etymology of ___

9. Upper Shiloh

UPPER SHILOH

I think Mother had a wild streak, but she acted rather proper most of the time. She had a calm, sort of dignified air about her. She impressed people without meaning to. When she was young she studied art in Germany. Then she came back and she married my father, a quarryman. We grew up in a house full of books. Now Mother was strict with Anna, whereas Dad, oh, I think he liked to spoil her. One summer Dad bought a 1949 Mercury from the widow of one of his workers. It was solid black, low and heavy and all curves, like a streamlined tank. What a beauty. Dad gave that car to Anna. There was a *scene* at the dinner table. Mother felt upstaged: "No, Bayard, no! I won't have it, she's too young, she's too . . . you know very well what she is!" And Father, always calm and reasonable, soothing her: "I reckon it will be all right, dear, I reckon it will be good for her, you'll see." In the end my mother backed down. Which was unusual for her. Since Wylie died, she'd gone a little flat. We were still trying to put the pieces together, each in our own way, trying to adjust to being only four now instead of five. Four was an uncomfortable number. We weren't used to the symmetry.

Maybe Dad believed the car was a way of reaching Anna. She was getting harder to handle. I can't say whether he succeeded or not, but my sister surely did love that old car. It made it possible for Anna to leave home that summer after her junior year at Buffalo City High School. My mother had a friend, Mrs. Shaughnessy, who lived about ten miles away, over in Chalybeate Springs, and she took in lodgers. Her house was built right up to the tracks. It used to be a railroad station at one time. They worked out an arrangement where Anna would live with Mrs. Shaughnessy and pay room and board. Anna would have to get a job. At least for the summer, until school started again. My parents were distraught. Seventeen-year-old girls didn't live alone in 1957. But in Anna's case they must have figured this would be their best hope of not losing her altogether.

From the very beginning railroads established a presence not only in the countryside but also in the territory of popular consciousness. In the thunderous drama of their arrivals and departures, appearing then disappearing al a narrow, uniform pathway, trains became conveyors of powerful symbolism. The "iron road" always seeks the Ideal Way: a straight and level passag through the unruly landscape. Its hal mark features, the broad curves and gentle gradients, are the product of a engineered compromise with topography. Railway tracks merge with and alter the terrain whenever they climb hill, bridge a stream, cross a viaduct, tunnel into a mountain or wind thro a city. Envisioning this network as a of specialized trails, a pattern of mea emerges, connecting us to landscape essential mystery. We are linked to th whole constellated system, in which even the lowliest trackside spot may l ennobled with a name, and every sta is a star . . .

Professor Elizabeth Vernon Meade, Uni Shenandoah, Dept. of Landscape Histor "Trackside." *Signal Lights* (Journal of th B & S Railroad Historical Society) 16 (M 1990): 27.

"From the very beginning, railroads established a presence not only in the countryside, but also within the territory of popular consciousness. In the thunderous drama of their arrivals and departures, appearing then disappearing along a narrow uniform pathway, trains became conveyers of powerful symbolism. The "iron road" always seeks the Ideal Way: a straight and level passage through the unruly landscape."

M. F.

Its hallmark features, the broad curves and gentle gradients, are the product of an engineered compromise with topography. Railway tracks merge with and alter the terrain wherever they climb a hill, bridge a stream, cross a viaduct, tunnel into a mountain or wind through a city. Envisioning this network as a map of specialized trails, a pattern of meaning emerges, connecting us to landscape's essential mystery. We are linked to the whole constellated system, in which even the lowliest track or spot may be ennobled with a name, and every station is like a star..."

~ Prof. Elizabeth V. Meade, Univ. of Shenandoah, Dept. of Social History. Trackside: Signal Light 6, (May 1990) p. 27, Journal of the B. & S. Railroad Historical Society.

10. Chalybeate Springs

Shenandoah straddles a winding river between steep hills. The city has an intricate, compacted feeling to it. Population about 50,000. Medina (rhymes with China) is a working-class section of mostly brick row houses and small factories. Medina and River City were separate towns originally, but as Shenandoah became more industrialized they were absorbed into the city, along with the western district of Euphrates, which was more residential. That was where the McKays lived and where Russell spent his childhood. A nice old neighborhood. I am not sure how much political autonomy these districts have any more, but all three at one time rated their own station stop on the B & S Railroad, and people still think of them as distinct places, even though you can't tell any more where one begins and the other leaves off.

At some point, going through the album, I realized there were a lot of water towers in Russell's pictures. Towers started showing up in the backgrounds, where I hadn't even noticed them before. Later I found this, in Russell's notebook:

Childhood memory: late afternoon, driving through Medina. Gas stations. Signs against the sky like heraldic emblems, star, sun, shell, crown, flying red horse. And railroad signs too, coming up to the B & S crossing on Queen Street, first the black X on the round yellow target, then the crossing sign by the tracks, white wooden X against dark sky. Look Out For Trains. Stop Look and Listen. Then over the crossing, a quick look down the tracks, semaphore signal on a pole, red and green lights. Telephone wires overhead, factories on Elgin Street catching the sun. Water towers above all: short ones, tall ones, alchemical vessels, retorts on girder legs, landmarks visible from afar, rising above the factory roofs high as church steeples, almost holy.

Me·di´na, n. **1.** mı-daı´nə; me-dī´na. A county in N. Ohio; 423 sq. m. **2.** Its county seat. **3.** A county in S. Texas; 1284 sq. m.; county seat, Hondo. **4.** A town in Appotomac Co., Virginia, contiguous with the city of Shenandoah but separately incorporated. **5.** A village in Orleans Co., N.Y. **6.** 1 mē-dī´na; 2 me-de´nä. A holy city in Hejas, Arabia 210 m. N.W. of Mecca; the goal of Mohammed's flight, or Hegira, in A.D. 622; and the place of his death, burial, and tomb: surrendered to King of Hedjaz Jan. 15, 1919.

James W. De Weems.
Names Upon the Land.
Baltimore, 1953.
[Appotomac County Athenaeum]

11. Medina

Me-di'na, n 1. 1 mi-dai'na; 2 me-di'na. A county in N. Ohio; 423 sq mi. 2. Its county seat.
3. a county in S Texas; 1284 sq mi; county seat Hon... 4. A town in Appotomac County, Virginia
contiguous with the city of Shenandoah, but separa... incorporated. 5. A village in Orleans County, New York
6. 1 me-di'na; me-di'na. A holy-city in Hejas, A'ra... mi. N.W. of Mecca; the goal of Mohammed's flight, or Hegira in
A.D. 622, and the place of his death, burial, and tomb; s... red to the king of Hedjaz Jan. 15, 1919.
— James. A. G. Names Upon The Land, Knoxville, 1915. ...e County Athenaeum).

MEDINA

If Russell McKay had a mission, it was to celebrate the grammar of ordinary places. Here and there we pause with him, along the railroad corridor, to catch an intimate glimpse of America's unofficial landscape, a haphazardly self-composed world, layered with the unattended mementos of passing time. (Professor Jordan Stillwell)

Stillwell had a theory about yards. Front yards are "dressed," he says, because they face the street, but backyards are naked. "Railroad space" is the backyard view. I was thinking of our own backyard in Buffalo City. Actually it was quite neat. We lived on a street of Federal-style row houses, built before the Civil War. It was Mother's idea of a nice neighborhood. Anna used to say it was "too nice." I liked it all right. The street was shady and clean and had cobblestone gutters. When Anna finished high school (she didn't exactly graduate), she had that old Mercury then, she left Mrs. Shaughnessy's and got herself an apartment at 24 Magnolia Street in River City and enrolled at the university. My father agreed to pay her tuition if she would help support herself. She got a job at the library. Anna loved that apartment. It was everything our old neighborhood wasn't. She felt free there. The streets were noisy and a little wild, and the yards were full of all kinds of interesting junk, and there was a family of colored people (as Mother called them) living upstairs. Anna was in heaven. About a year later she moved to a bigger place around the corner at 149 Java, three blocks from the tracks, that had a separate back room she could use for a studio. Anna stayed in that place about fifteen years.

Anna lives by the river, a short walk from Alleghany Avenue, where the o trolley line still runs downtown into Shenandoah. Most mornings she rid the streetcar into the city, to her job a the library, trundling along past buil ings from whose windows women on waved to the gray-clad men of Jubal Early's cavalry. Sometimes she day-dreams, gazing at the passing façades shadow under tiers of wooden balcon hung with laundry, imagining some scene of love or bondage in a shabby half-lit room, without poetry, a hidde life indoors, more authentic than her own. One morning she stays home, having hired a carpenter to make sor repairs in the apartment. At lunchtin she gives the man beer and sandwich eat. They sit together in the kitchen v the windows open. A factory whistle sounds in the noon distance. Later w the man has gone, she finds a folded paper with his message, a map of the kitchen floor, marked with a treasure cross. X marks the spot. Alone that ni her memory swims in an oceanic im of discarded clothes, floating around them like islands on the shimmering sun-dappled floor . . .

Journal of Anna B. (c. 1959?). [Shenand Public Library]

M · F ·

12. River City

Anna lives by the river, a short walk from Allegheny Avenue; A trolley line takes her along the avenue downtown into Shenandoah, to the city library where she works. A dusty orange streetcar trundles down the tracks past rows of buildings from whose windows (it is documented) women once waved to the grey-clad men of Jubal A. Early's cavalry. Anna daydreams on this ride. Her eyes search the passing facades, now in shadow under tiers of balconies, stairways, and open porches hung with laundry. She invents a hidden indoors world unburdened by poetry, imagining scenes of love and bondage in shabby half-lit rooms. One morning she stays home while a carpenter works on her apartment. At lunch time they sit together in the kitchen with the windows open and drink beer and eat sandwiches. A factory whistle sounds off in the noon distance. Later the carpenter leaves a note for her to find, a map-like drawing of the kitchen, with a treasure cross at the center. Where the polished tiles melt away, X marks the spot. There she reflects. Her memory swims in an oceanic image of discarded clothes, like islands, floating around them on the shimmering, sun-dappled floor.

From the journals of Anna B. (c. 1959?), p. 144. — Shenandoah Public Library.

RIVER CITY

Until 1950 the B & S maintained a small station at Baltimore Street, a mile north of the downtown depot. I remember it was like a gingerbread cottage, cream color with green trim. A few years ago someone converted it into a Chinese restaurant. In the late 1940s Russell's father used to board the train there to go off on his business trips.

Russell went to the Park Elementary School on Euphrates Avenue, ten blocks from where the McKays lived. He used to tell us about running to the schoolyard fence, to watch the B & S steam engines go chugging through the ravine down below. Only there was so much foliage he couldn't see the train, just a huge column of smoke coming up, moving through the trees. Anna asked him once, did you ever sit by the tracks and wait for trains? No, he said, I *never* did that. I guess it never occurred to him. Train encounters had to be a matter of luck. Russell wrote that the railroad seemed "incongruously intimate" then:

The B & S brings with it an aura of countryside as it makes its secret way into town, crossing the city limits north of the Powhatan Country Club, skirting golf courses and lacrosse fields, south along Cold Spring Creek through a green sanctuary of interconnected parks, cemeteries and school grounds: Sacred Heart Convent, Hawthorn, Mt. Olivet Park, Calvert Academy, St. Barnabas, Friends School. It takes a hide-and-seek course through a cut behind the elementary school playground, then continues alongside the rear fences of graceful yards, shielded from view of the houses behind a running border of hedges, mimosa trees, ornamental shrubs and wild vines, disappearing under University Parkway through a massive vaulted stone arch blackened with soot from the passing of locomotives below street level, invisible from the avenues above. Skirting the edge of Shenandoah University, the railroad winds into another leafy ravine, Franklin Park, behind the Museum of Art, with its walkways and flowers and statues and trickling fountains. Finally it disappears in a tunnel under Baltimore Street. Half a block further, beneath a gigantic billboard, the sunken tracks emerge from the darkness. The railroad levels out in a narrow freight yard by the riverbank, among the cinders and weeds of the roundhouse area and cobbled streets crammed with warehouses and small factories, the very heart of Shenandoah.

There are five station stops within Shenandoah city limits, including the branch line to Euphrates and the contiguous incorporated townships of River City and Medina. A short drive leads home, from Baltimore Street Station, past brick factory buildings with water towers, over an asphalt street crisscrossed with railroad sidings. Going north the pavement narrows. The street, winding past ancient stone mills, is hemmed in by rock walls and banks of ailanthus (Tree of Heaven), whose palmy leaves cast tropical shadows along the deep-cut road. In this compact valley, in the heart of the city, the margins between lush nature and neglected industry are undefined. It has the exotic, fertile aura of a no-man's-land.

There are five stations within Shenandoah city limits (including the branch line to Euphrates) and the contiguous incorporated townships of River City and Medina. The drive north will take us home, from Baltimore Street station past brick and stone factories, over asphalt street criss-crossed with railroad sidings. Going north the street narrows, winding past ancient stone mills, hem...in by rock walls and ailanthus trees whose palmy leaves cast tropical shadows along the deep cut road; a compac...lley where the margins between industry and nature dissolve into each other to create a lawless and m...ous no-man's land.

13. Baltimore Street

BALTIMORE STREET

Shenandoah University occupies a steep hill near the center of town. When I first showed the album to Professor Stillwell we met at his office in Zion Hall. You can see the whole city from up there. It was cloudy that morning. Stillwell mentioned that Zion Hall was one of the few buildings left standing after the Union Army bombarded the school.* I told him that his building was made of limestone blocks quarried by my great-great-grandfather Tayloe Murphy Caton in 1850. I liked Stillwell. We talked about the city. He said Shenandoah was "a repository for anachronism." (*Like Russell*, I thought.) It's true, if you go back only twenty years ago, you'll be stumbling all over the past. Say you were to walk down Euclid Street, by Ike's Candy Store. Headlines in *The Shenandoah Gazette*: Vietnam, men on the moon. *The Godfather* is showing at the Majestic, the only building in the block that's not a hundred years old. A horse-drawn vegetable wagon weaves through the downtown traffic. At Fairfax, you stroll under the arcade of the City Produce Market, unchanged since the Civil War. Cross Alleghany Avenue. A dark green streetcar (streamlined in 1935) clatters along the median, trolley pole skimming and sparking under the wires. Those car tracks were laid in 1910. Turn off onto Marypen Street. Three blocks east and you come to the railroad, the B & S terminal: freight yards wedged in by the river, ancient sheds, engine facilities, water and coal, the brick roundhouse, dark entrances curving round an eighty-foot turntable, where the huge engines (steam locomotives until 1961) are rotated, to line up with their stalls. Mr. McKay used to drive by this way, for Russell's sake, on their way home after Sunday school.

After my meeting with Stillwell, I drove over to Marypen Street, and I parked by the tracks. The old roundhouse is still in use; they keep diesels there now. A ray of sunlight broke through the clouds just as a freight train came into view. I stayed there in my truck in that patch of sunlight, and I listened to that slow train clanging and squealing and rattling and groaning . . . I watched it roll on past me, right down the line, until the dust settled and the last car passed out of sight.

*In August of 1862, General Omar Blackburn McLean's Union Army laid siege to Shenandoah. The Federals established temporary headquarters at the heavily damaged college, whose misfortune it was to be situated on a scenic but strategically important rise near the downtown area.

City, temple, theater, planetarium, obelisk, library, tabernacle, hall of industry, archive, fountain, acropolis, dome, palace of art, sphinx, park, botanical gardens, oasis, reservoir, channel, aqueduct, canal, water tower, telephone poles, alley, boulevard, overpass, billboard, newsstand, lunch counter, workshop, factory, smokestack, power lines, oil tank, chimney, warehouse, central terminal, depot, crossing, illuminated signals, semaphore, rail junction, trackage, viaduct, bridge, trestle, embankment, stone retaining wall, culvert, masonry, archway, underpass, portal, tunnel, bore, passage, track, smoke, locomotive, vapor, haze, engine, steam, sulphur, ashes, cinders, rust, corrosion, disappearance, departure, darkness.

Russell grew up in Euphrates. We never visited the McKays, because of a family feud. Their house was in an old neighborhood with winding streets and trees and hedges and flowers. Russell used to play with his toy soldiers in the backyard, around the roots of a sycamore tree. There was a particular root that rose up like an island: Guadalcanal. Whole battalions fought and died there. Funny, this deep feeling for World War II. Russell and I had that in common, even though I was a few years younger. His father and my father both fought the Nazis. But for some reason, we agreed, the Pacific war was more thrilling. Oh, Europe was all right, and we admired Rommel in the desert, but the *Pacific* . . . Those names! Every kid knew them like a catechism. Pearl Harbor, Guam, Okinawa, Wake, Corregidor, the Solomons, Guadalcanal, Iwo Jima, Coral Sea, Leyte, Midway, Bataan. We had movies, of course, and comics to inspire us. We fought elaborate air battles with fighter planes made from Monogram kits: Zeros, Hellcats, Thunderbolts, Corsairs, Mustangs. We'd spend whole rainy days indoors building those balsa wood models. They flew (and burned) spectacularly. Even now, just remembering the sweet toxic smell of model-airplane paint (Testor's Dope) . . . it makes me think of the Pacific Ocean.

After Russell's funeral, we got it into our heads to go by the McKays' old house. Anna had the address. Whoever lived there wasn't home. We let ourselves into the backyard through the alley gate. We found the sycamore tree, still standing. One root bigger than the rest. We sat there for a minute, on Guadalcanal. I was sort of poking around at the grass, not thinking of anything. I turned over a clump of moss and I felt something. It was a little painted metal figure, corroded and caked in dirt. You could see the U.S. Marine helmet, and the arms bent holding a rifle, and one leg missing. I showed Anna. Did you have a *feeling?* she said.

A system of connected woods and meadows extends south into Trinidad Park, infusing the orderly old resident neighborhoods of western Shenandoa with nature and wildness through a miniature primeval valley. The tainte waters of Euphrates Creek flow down through parklands in lazy meanders, sometimes hemmed in by borders of tile along the adjacent backyards. Following these curves, here and the angling across over stone culverts, a railroad track runs alongside the strea The Euphrates branch of the Buffalo Shenandoah Railroad threads throug the length of the park as discreetly as the creek itself, by way of tangents an curves. The rails are rusty from infrequent use. The wood cross ties are splintered, weathered gray, embedde in the weed-grown cinder ballast. In many places the crumbling roadbed pears indistinguishable from the mos earth. Only the parallel rails, visible above the grass and wildflowers, sugg that this is not some path of nature b conduit of industry, a channel for co oil, furniture, grain, limestone, milk, perishable fruit and the products of distant factories.

M F

15. Euphrates

...m of connected woods and meadows extends south into Trinidad Park, infusing the orderly old residential ...borhoods of northern Shenandoah with Nature and wildness, through a miniature primeval valley. Here the ... of Euphrates Creek flow down through parklands in lazy meanders or tumble + tebbinks along backyard borders. ... curves, or angling across it over stone culverts & railroad ties ... alongside the stream. It threads through the park, ... Buffalo and Shenandoah Railway (... branch) as ... Creek itself, by way tangents and gentle curves. ... rails are rusty from ... use. The wood ... are spattered and weathered grey, embedded in the weedgrown ... gravel and cinders ... some places the crumbled roadbed appears indistinguishable from the mossy earth, so that only ... rising above grass and wildflowers suggest that this is not one of Nature's paths but a conduit of industry, a channel ... coal, furniture, limestone, milk, perishable fruit, and the promise of distant factories.

EUPHRATES

Damascus Junction is no town any more, only a place on the railroad map with two different names, depending on the railroad. The Powhatan track begins here at a switch off the B & S. It curves west, then climbs along the creek and up into the mountains. The station probably takes its name from the old Damascus Road, which crosses the B & S at this point. This was a favorite hangout of Russell's. Lots of switching activity here, between the two lines.

The B & S was running new diesels by the mid-1960s while the Powhatan Railroad continued along in the Stone Age: the Powhatan still kept some big steam locomotives in service around Egypt and up north at the mines. Now and then one of those engines might show up at the junction, to switch cars at the interchange. Russell said Damascus was where time zones seemed to overlap. To find a working steam engine then was like catching sight of green leaves on a tree in November.*

In 1965 Bob Dylan came out with *Highway 61 Revisited*, and Martin Luther King marched on Selma, Alabama; I was away at college in Baltimore. Vietnam was heating up and Andy Warhol was becoming famous. Imagine, steam and smoke on the Powhatan, overlapping with Andy Warhol. The last call came on a snowy day in February of that year (according to an article in the *Shenandoah Gazette*) when a Powhatan locomotive delivered twenty-five loaded coal cars to the B & S siding at Damascus. The engine steamed thirty miles back up to the mine with a train of empties. At the end of that run they dumped the fires out of her, and it was all over.

*A handful of American railroads, such as the Lake Superior & Ishpeming, Colorado & Southern, Louisiana Eastern, Duluth Missabe & Iron Range, Magma Arizona, Buffalo Creek & Gauley, and the narrow-gauge Denver & Rio Grande Western, still operated steam locomotives into the 1960s.

junc′tion, 1 juŋk′shən; 2 jŭṉe′shon, n. . . . 2. A place of union; point of meeting; joint; specif., a spot or static where railroads meet or intersect: oft used as a place-name; as, Damascus *Junction*. [< L. junctio (n.), < jungo, join].

Da-mas′cus, 1 də-mas′kus; 2 da-măs′ n. [L.] 1. A district in Syria, between Lebanon and the Euphrates. 2. An ancient city in Syria; possessed succe sively by Hebrews, Assyrians, Persian Macedonians, Romans, Saracens and Turks, captured by British Oct. 2, 19 3. A town in Early Co., Georgia (po 402); in Montgomery Co., Maryland (pop. 1000); in Wayne Co., Pennsylvania (pop. 300); in Mahoning Co., Arkansas (pop. 80); in Appotomac C Virginia (pop. 20).

ion; a junk´shan; z; ...e shon, n ...2. A place of union; point of meeting;
nt; specif; a spot a station where railroads meet or intersect: often used as a place name, as in
itle River Junction. [< L junctio (n), < jungo, join.]

16. Damascus Junction

mas´cus; 1 da-mas´kus); ... da-mäs´ĕŭs, n. [L.] 1. A district in Syria; possessed successively by Hebrews, Assyrians,
...donians Romans, Saracens, and Ottoman Turks, captured by British Oct. 2, 1918 3. A town in Early County,
...ontgomery County; Maryland (pop. 1000); in Wayne Co., Pennsylvania (pop. 300); in Mahoning Co., Ohio (pop. 700);
...Co. Arkansas, (pop. 30); in Shenanooh Co. Parthenia (pop. 200).

DAMASCUS JUNCTION

Mt. Zion takes its name from an old country church. There's a Gulf station, a general store and a post office. I never heard about any tunnel in that area until I saw the picture. I was up by Mt. Zion about a month ago because a farmer over there had an old Ford tractor advertised for sale. Their name was Stickley. His wife asked me in. I said, do you know anything about a railroad tunnel near here?

"Yes sir," said Mr. Stickley, "it starts right at the end of our cornfield, down in the ravine."

I asked would it be all right if I walked over there to take a look.

"Honey," Mrs. Stickley said, "you don't want to go down there."

I said, "Why?"

"Snakes," she said. "There was a young man came through here about twenty years ago, remember him, Lyndon? and he wanted to see *that tunnel*. And he had a big camera with him. Lyndon, my husband, said all right now, but mind, you be careful. Well, it was about four hours later, and to tell the truth I'd forgotten about that boy. Then I saw him. Coming up through the cow lot. He was pale and reeling like, and one pants leg rolled up, the leg all swollen. *I got bit by a rattlesnake*, he said. Well, I got on the phone to Memorial Hospital. He weren't in no shape to drive himself and so Lyndon drove him into town. He was right sick but they saved him. He came by a few days later to fetch his camera, which he'd left, and he thanked us. I asked him what was you doing down there anyway? *Taking pictures of trains*, he said. Can you beat that? Taking pictures of trains! Now what *was* his name? I don't recollect. McCoy? McCabe? Lord almighty, I'll tell you if it wasn't for Lyndon's fast driving, the boy would have been dead as a hammer. And that's a fact."

Zi´on, 1 zai´en; 2 zi´on, n. 1. Bib. A ⬚ in Jerusalem, which after the captur⬚ that city from the Jebusites became ⬚ royal residence of David and his suc⬚ cessors; hence, the ancient Hebrew theocracy: "Nevertheless, Dā´vid too⬚ the stronghold of Zi´on: The same a⬚ City of Dā´vid." 2 *Sam.* v.7. [< Gr. ⬚ [Hebr. *Tsiyon*, hill]. 2. The heavenl⬚ Jerusalem; heaven. 3. A town in Ma⬚ Co., Illinois (pop. 438); in Van Bur⬚ Co., Iowa (pop. 50); in Wilkes Co.,⬚ N. Carolina (pop. 100); in Calhoun⬚ W. Virginia (pop. 25); in Appotoma⬚ Co., Virginia (pop. 64).

James Walker Taliaferro.
Place-Names and their Origins.
Buffalo City, 1929. [Shenandoah Public⬚ Library]

17. Mt. Zion

Zi'on, 1 zai'en; 2 zī'on, n. 1. Bib. A hill in Jerusalem, which after the capture of that city from the Jebusites became the royal residence of David and his successors; hence the ancient Hebrew theocracy. "Nevertheless David took the stronghold of Zi'on. The same is the City of Da'vid." (2 Sam. v.7.] 2. The heavenly Jerusalem; heaven. 3. A town in Macon County, Ill. (pop. 438); in Van Buren County, Iowa (pop. 50); in Walker County N. Carolina (pop. 100); in Calhoun County, W. Virginia (pop. 25); in Appotowac County, Virginia (pop. 64).

~ Talliaferro. Walter E. Place Names and their Origins. Buffalo City. 1929. (Shenandoah Public Library).

We come to these stations just as if we were riding on a train, one after the other, turning the pages, following the fixed line of the railroad map. That was the sequence Russell decided on. It *seems* obvious; but maybe it's not so obvious. There's a lot of ruminating in Russell's notes, about "time" and "place":

We usually think of places as existing on a plane, approachable from any direction. On the other hand, time is supposed to flow along in a continuous line. We can only look back at time. It's like the rear view from the last car of a moving train, where you watch the tracks slipping away under you, converging in the distance, and the space between the rails is uniform, and the ties are spaced evenly, like our days, helping to measure, and the telephone poles like months or weeks, set at breathing intervals, but regular, passing, everything passing . . . receding . . .

But in the album, time is more "spatial." Anna goes every which-a-way in time and all I can do is follow her, and so there's no chronology. More like an open field. All these fragments together are not exactly my idea of a story. Wylie used to tease me at the dinner table, how I always ate one thing at a time. I prefer it that way, is all. Things in proper order. Actually, I suspect that this need to arrange and organize objects is a sign of mental *dis*order. I mean chaos. I'm not a clear thinker. I've known and admired people who are clear thinkers, who can live in the middle of every kind of goddamn disarray and it doesn't bother them. In fact, not only do they not mind it . . . and this is the killer . . . they don't even *notice* it.

Like the ancient hedgerows of Engla the railroad right-of-way has become miniature linear environment, a path way through the larger landscape as as a landscape unto itself. Along one runs a drainage ditch . . . cattails gro the standing water, which may harb not only frogs but large fish like bull heads and carp. Cardinal flowers an purple loosestrife climb its gravelly banks. The level roadbed, built to a slightly higher profile than the fields through which it passes, is flanked b row of telephone poles. On a hot, st day the wires hum. The motionless smells of metal and creosote. Polishe rails shimmer, receding into the dis- tance. The nine-inch space betweer cross ties is uncomfortable for walki This is company property, yet it ma well be yours, or belong to no one . a domain without inhabitants, a zon beyond the usual accepted notions bodily and moral safety . . .

Professor J. S. *The Zone.*
Shenandoah University Press, 1981.
"A contemporary study of the cultural, topographic and aesthetic aspects of railroad space." [Appotomac County Athenaeum]

18. Blueville

"Like the ancient hedge rows of England, the railroad right-of-way has become a miniature environment, a pathway through the larger landscape, as well as a landscape unto itself. Along one side runs a drainage ditch — cattails grow in the standing water which may harbor not only frogs, but fish, occasionally bullhead and carp. Cardinal flowers and purple loosestrife climb its gravelly banks. The leveled roadbed, built to maintain a slightly higher profile than the fields through which it passes, is flanked by a row of telephone poles. On hot, still days the wires hum. The motionless air smells of metal and creosote. Polished rails shimmer as recede into the distance. You cannot quite walk comfortably along the nine-inch space between the rows of cross-ties. This is Company property, yet it may or will belong to you or to no one ... a domain with no inhabitants, a zone beyond the usual and accepted notions of bodily and moral safety."

[From The Zone, by Professor J. S., Shenandoah University Press, 1981 — A contemporary study of the cultural, aesthetic and topographic aspects of railroad-space in the American landscape.]

Appotomac County Atheneum, Buffalo City, W. Va.

BLUEVILLE

Our grandpa Jerome married a city girl named Wanda Levitzky. She died in the great flu epidemic of 1919 when Daddy was eleven. Then Jerome Caton married Miss Ellen, our step-grandma, and they lived for a while at Luray Run. My brother Wylie used to love to sleep on that big back porch.

There was a fellow by the name of A. G. Evans that Russell told me about. Everyone called him A. G., and he had a pretty high-up job on the B & S. It happened that he and my father were classmates in high school. He was one of the initial backers of Russell's project. (Evans was an enthusiast as well as a business-man, and a founder of the B & S Railroad Historical Society, which exists today.) According to Russell, it wouldn't be uncommon, on a small railroad like this, for the managers to sometimes ride with the train crews. Most of them came up through the ranks. Evans started as a signal maintainer. Anyway, I have the news-paper here, it was August 13, 1975. A. G. Evans was riding in the caboose of a freight local heading south for Manassah. It was a dark night. They say Evans was dozing. The train came to an unscheduled stop, with the rear end of the train parked out on that Luray Run bridge sixty-five feet above the creek. Apparently Evans woke up and he jumped straight out of that caboose, to see what was wrong. There was a lot wrong. They recovered his body from the creek bed the next morning.

In back of his grandparents' house trellises covered in ivy nearly enclose the wooden second-story porch, whi offers a privileged view in bare early spring of the trestle over Luray Run. this place as if on a stage, the railroa displays its antiquated structures and equipment. Here steam locomotives continue to impinge upon the mode world: big grimy engines that devou coal and water, that fill the air with spectacular exhalations, embodying zenith of mechanical power. But be so visibly fiery, so fragrant, huge and clamorous in their comings and goi masks an awful fragility, their precar state in time. Perhaps it is some dim sense of this impending extinction th provokes the anxious pleasure, the u easy excitement, a hunger to see and collect visions and proofs, so that fra ments at least might survive, to lodg memory's suspect terrain . . . like the roadside history markers denoting si of past endeavor, of birth, settlemen battle and exploration.

Essay by Wylie Ray Caton (age 16). Submitted by Anna B. Caton to *The Valley Herald* in 1979 (unpublished).

LURAY RUN

A plate girder railroad bridge crosses the Valley Pike north of Marveltown. It's one of the few B & S bridges you can see where the whole name is spelled out. Maybe that's why Russell wanted that picture for *Stations*. He did take other photographs of the town. One print I saw, I'll never forget, it showed the Athenaeum shrouded in mist like a Greek temple. (That's the one I would have chosen.)

A long time ago Russell was involved with some woman who (I believe) worked at the Athenaeum. I don't know her name. My story is full of holes. All he ever said was it was history. I think she got pregnant and she didn't want to marry Russell. She must have brought up that child alone. I never dared asked Russell about it. You got the feeling it was a dark secret. Or painful, anyway. So that could be why he didn't care to use the Athenaeum photo.

There's another possibility, and it has to do with Anna. After all, these pages come from her. Did she decide what to include or exclude? There is no other intact album to use for comparison. The images have been colored, and sometimes changed so much that, as Professor Stillwell says, we can't always be sure what we've got. It becomes more puzzling, not less. Sometimes I find myself wondering, whose pictures are these after all? *And what exactly are they?*

One thing, as I've said, Anna was always altering things. It became another family joke (thanks mostly to Wylie), like the way I would eat only one thing at a time. Once Anna got a brand-new purse from somebody. She got some lye out from under the kitchen sink and she dipped the clasp in that to dull the metal. Too bright, she said. She preferred things that looked old. But if they came from somewhere else, like India or China, they might be all right. I remember another time Daddy bought Momma a new toaster. It had fake wood grain on the sides, which my sister found very disturbing. Well, she went after it with steel wool and paint remover. She wrecked the toaster. She caught hell for that one. When she got older, almost every book she owned, she'd make a new cover for it. As I say, Anna was always inventing, always making herself up.

Starting at the reservoir, Canal Road brings you through a one-way tunnel to the park. Follow Garden Drive, as far as the art museum. Bear right at t fountain. Stay on Alleghany Avenue, past the Majestic Theater, all the wa down to the freight yards at the unde pass. You'll see some oil tanks on the other side and a big flying red horse. Head right onto Egypt Street. Go on block, then left at the piano factory. Damascus Road leads straight out of town. It's a two-lane highway about miles down the valley, as far as Luray Run. Marveltown is 2 more miles. Watch for the battlefield markers. G left on Innes Street, just before the bridge. Continue across the tracks. Turn right on Parthenia. After a row elms, you'll see an old dust-colored Greek Revival building with colum That's the Athenaeum. Go directly the marble stairs. Ask for Sophia.

Written instructions.

SHENANDOAH

M. F.

20. Marveltown

Starting at the reservoir, Canal Road brings you through a one-way tunnel into the park. Follow Garden Drive, as far as the Art Museum. Bear right at the fountain. Stay on Alleghany Avenue, past the Majestic Theater, all the way down to the freight yards at the underpass. You'll see some oil tanks on the other side, and a big flying red horse. Head right, onto Egypt Street. Go one block, then left at the piano factory. Damascus Road leads straight out of town. It's a two-lane highway, about 10 miles down the valley, as far as Luray Run. Marveltown is 2 more miles. Watch for the battlefield markers. Go left on Dinas Street, just before the bridge. Continue across the tracks. Turn right on Parthenia. After a row of elms, you'll see an old dust-colored Greek Revival building with columns. That's the Atheneum. Go directly up the marble stairs. Ask for Sophia.

—Written Instructions

MARVELTOWN

Years ago Russell used to work for a carpenter in Shenandoah named Harley Peyton, who I reckon was quite a character. I remember his name only because Russell was always telling Harley Peyton stories. One weekend Harley was helping a nephew of his lay some four-inch sewer pipe in the nephew's backyard. It was a fairly new house in the bottomland down near Easter Creek. They were digging by hand, a straight narrow trench. All of a sudden Harley's shovel struck something that made a little clanging sound. It was a Confederate belt buckle. Then they found some brass buttons, all in a row. Then a little hair, they said. Nothing else. No bones, no nothing. They kept digging on that tangent, and they came across another grouping like the first. Harley unearthed eleven "bodies" all told, perfectly lined up in the direction he happened to be digging. Eleven sets of buttons. It must have been a whole Confederate burial ground. There had been some fierce fighting around there in 1864. Of course you could say *that* about nearly every yard and cow pasture in the valley.

Harley should have notified the authorities, but he didn't. The state would have put up a big kick about it and sent a swarm of archaeologists in there with their tweezers and their little brushes and all, and maybe they would have detected the bones that way, but Harley's nephew would never have gotten that quiet little patio he wanted. So they went ahead and laid flagstones when they were done with the pipe. Put in a terrace over the whole damn plot. Never said what was under there.

MF

21. Easter Creek

Near this place at dawn, on October 2, 1864, troops of Painter and
Beauregard under C. Meaning ____ ____ to attack the Union Army, which ____
in an entrenched camp close to the banks, defended by Major Braintree. Braintree's men,
pursued by Meaning, were hampered in their retreat due to having burned the bridge.
—— State Historical Marker

The company that my father worked for most of his life owned several quarries in the valley. One was at Lima. When he was first married, he started out there as a foreman. Wylie was born there. But then they ran out of good limestone and they closed the pit in 1940 and Dad was transferred up to Buffalo City. Lima had one of the oldest quarries around. There are six old quarries in a row down that way. One of them is still active. The others are located south of Lima at the junction. If I didn't know all these places were actually there, along the railroad, I'd be tempted to wonder if Russell didn't invent them: so many of his images have to do with *digging* in some way. And there is that sand pit near Chinaville, and a coal mine up at Powhatan. Russell himself was a digger. Always talking about *places*, and "excavating" the past, and how people should slow down in order to experience things and feel things properly. Sometimes in the diary, you get a sense of Russell trying to sort these things out:

Today [1976] we whiz from place to place. No time to resonate. To experience the truth of a place it takes patience (which we don't have) and work (which we don't want to do). You have to dig. Modern life opposes this kind of perception. People say it's better to "live in the moment." But they don't mean it, not in any deep sense. Their so-called moment is really nothing but chaos and distraction. Impossible to experience places (or pictures either) without engaging in time. *We don't value the past, not truly, except to sentimentalize it. People think it must be depressing to hang around the railroad taking pictures of shabby old buildings. But it's just the opposite. The work is one thing that uplifts me.*

No-man's-land, eyesore, wasteland, p hole in the ground, excavation, open wound. Mine, rock quarry, depths, secret beauty, subtraction, exposure, cutaway view, danger zone, crater, revelation, blight on the land, precip gaping mouth, netherworld, furrow, gash, aperture, mystery spot, abyss, re pository of yearning, gateway of desir pillaged terrain, pocket, hollow, sour concavity, spring, subterranean pool, mineral, fossil, magnet, symbol . . .

Settlement, cluster, home place, mic cosm, hamlet, man's world, abiding place, dot on the map, accumulation memory, history, small town, village, house, store, yards, alleys, trees, telephone poles, water tower, church steeple, faith, commerce, desire, play ground, network of trails, billboards, roadside markers, cemetery, family names, place-name, station stop, rail road crossing, off the beaten track, h town, middle of nowhere . . .

M. F.

No-man's land, eyesore, wasteland, pit, hole in the ground, excavation, open wound, mine, rock quarry, de... secret beauty, subtraction, exposure, cut-away view d... gone, crater, revelation, blight on the land, precipice, gaping... nether world, furrow, gash, aperture, mystery... epository of yearning, gateway of desire, pillaged terrain, po... source, concavity, spring, subterranean pool, mineral, fossil... symbol...

Settle... ...neplace, microcosm, **22. Lima**
hamlet... ...t of the map, named place,
accreti... ...e of memories, town hall, brick house,
back... ...telephone poles, water tower, church
stee... ...tboards, roadside markers, railroad
cro... ...ool hall, barber shop, tavern, soda fountain,
e exchange, safe haven, burial ground...

LIMA

The junction is a nondescript place on the outskirts of Manassah, where the B & S meets the Southern Railroad. Recently I had to go down that way, to take care of some farm business. Afterwards I drove around to the junction. I was curious to see where Russell's photograph came from. Well, I found the exact spot. Twenty years later it looks about the same. Just some cast-off corner of the landscape where nobody (excepting Russell) would ever think to take a picture. If I'd been asked before to describe that place, where five quarries used to be, I'd say there's *nothing* there. No reason to stop, unless maybe to read the history marker at the side of the road. The sign mentions James Caton, who was a brother of Elijah Mann Caton, one of my ancestors. It's surrounded by poison ivy now, and the cast iron is rust-stained and the silver and black paint is flaking off. I remember we used to talk about those signs, wondering who it was who initially wrote them all, those on-the-spot history lessons. Russell copied into his diary, word for word, "the anonymous poetry" of some of his favorite signs, which usually began in a similar way: On this site . . . Here stood the house . . . Near this spot . . . This place was named . . . Across the road . . . A short distance north . . . At this point . . . This site was where . . . and so on. Proof of the past. That's what Russell always seemed to be looking for:

This valley [is] defined by its epic Civil War battles. To me the most evocative [history markers] describe ordinary moments: "General So-and-So rested here before crossing the river." The past becomes suddenly palpable, more human. The frequent use of that simple word "here" moves me as much as anything. It allows you, the roadside traveler, to realize that you now are also "here," pausing to read, as you breathe the air of this place, in contemplation of some past event.

Formerly Caton's Grove, deeded to James Caton in 1762, this site was sacred to the Shawnee Indians. Beginning in 1840 limestone was quarried here and transported to the Capital, where it was used in the construction many imposing monuments and buildings. The stone blocks were hauled by mule wagon along the Valley Pike to Shenandoah, and from thence to Harpersburg, to be unloaded into boats on the Potomac Canal. Jackson's army which was destroying railroads to defend The Valley from Northern invasion, paused at this place in March 1862. Following The Conflict, two rail lines joined here in 1867, thereafter greatly furthering the limestone production. Nearby stand the walls of the original Caton house, burned by Union soldiers in 1865.

Roadside marker,
Appotomac County.

23. White Stone Junction.

Formerly Caton's Grove, deeded to James Caton in 1762, this site was ... sacred ... where ... over the Shawnee Indians.
Beginning in 1840 limestone was quarried here, and transported to the Capit... ... my which used in the construction of many imposing monuments and buildings. The stone blocks were hauled by mule wagon ... Pike to Shenandoah, and from thence to Harpersburg, to be unloaded into boats of the Potomac Canal. Jackson ... walls of ... destroying railroads to defend the Valley from Northern invasion, paused at this place in March, 1862. ... rail lines established a junction here, thereafter furthering a great increase in the lime production. Nearby stand ... ton house, burned by Sheridan's men in 1865.

— Appotomac County Roadside Marker #267

WHITE STONE JUNCTION

Manassah is the end of the line on the B & S. I got my first job in this town. Also my first apartment. I was fresh out of school, working on *The Valley Herald*. It was the mid-sixties. I stayed a couple of years. It was just then that Anna and Russell went on a train trip to New York. Russell had been to school up there, and maybe worked in the city for a while too, I forget. Anyway, he knew some art gallery people, and he wanted to help Anna make connections. This is the letter she wrote me from New York:

4 May, 1966. The Hotel Earle, Greenwich Village

Oh Lucky Dear Lucky,
At last I am showing slides of my work to some people here which makes me feel as good as I should, thanks to R. and today it rained alternately in different parts of the city so that if you were talking on the telephone to someone a few blocks away they were having rain and you weren't or vice versa. I am fine. R. introduced me to a famous art dealer who is very gentlemanly and who said very encouraging things about my work. Tomorrow we are taking the train up to New Haven to see Walker Evans who teaches I think at Yale and who is very old and who is without a doubt Russell's all-time hero and the greatest photographer who ever lived. R. and I caused a sensation in the Automat by complaining when the chocolate milk machine wouldn't pour and the man behind the machine was dubious about whether we had put our nickels in and a crowd collected and several people pounded it and finally like a shy awkward cow it gave forth and we were vindicated and so was it. I think you are destined to become a great WRITER, m'dear, tho' why in God's name you'd want to live in Manassah is beyond me. Even home (ugh) wd be better. Keep yr sights set on higher places and don't let small-town-itis keep you from it. R. is sexy and charming and says he loves me, but his eye always seems to be on something distant (a train?). As for me, I don't say such words, it's a little scary to be in love with someone as crazy as him, so I just take it from day to day.

love Anna

Named for a chief of the Appotomac Indians, a Shawnee tribe, whose home place was here. Founded in 1743, the town was situated in Lord Fairfax's proprietary of the Northern Neck. The earthworks on the hilltop to the south west were constructed by General Ba in the campaign of 1862. On May 24 one-half mile south of here, Stonewa Jackson attacked the Union forces, in retreat along the Valley Pike (present day Route 11), forcing Banks to divid his army.

Road sign, state historical marker no. A-23.

Ancient burial place, believed by stat archaeologists to be the tomb of Chie Manassah, unearthed in 1957 near Taliaferro's limestone quarry at the Southern Railroad junction. There is now a stone obelisk to mark the site.

M. F.

24. Manassah

Named for a chief of the Appotomac Indians, a Shawnee tribe, whose homeplace was here. Founded in 1743, the town was situated in Lord Fairfax's proprietary of the Northern Neck. The earthworks on the hilltop to the west were constructed by General Banks in the campaign of 1862. On May 24, one-half mile south of here, Stonewall Jackson attacked the Union forces in retreat along the Valley Pike (present day Route 11), forcing Banks to divide his army.
— Roadside Historical Marker

Ancient burial places, believed by state archeologists to be the tomb of Chief Manassah, unearthed in 1957 near Tuckahoe's handsome quarry at the Southern RR junction. There is more stone below to mark the site.

APPOTOMAC COUNTY ATHENEUM

MANASSAH

THE
POWHATAN
RAILROAD

One time Anna brought Russell along to our parents' house for Thanksgiving dinner. Russell and Anna had just been up to the spa hotel at Camden Springs. Mom and Dad actually stayed once at that same hotel, on a lark, before the war. We were all sitting around the table, polishing off the turkey. Mother got to reminiscing about the Springs. Mineral baths. Picnics on the lawn. Tennis. The old hotel was "dry," but they managed to sneak some booze and a highball shaker into their room. The spa reminded her of Germany, where she studied art one summer. Anna said, oh, Momma, you've got to tell Russell your *story*. Mother blushed, but she enjoyed being persuaded. This is her story, which Anna and I already knew by heart:

"It was 1935. I was about twenty-three. The art school was near a famous spa. I had a young German beau, his name was Franz. A very sensitive boy. His parents were communists. Franz and I used to bicycle over to the hotel sometimes on Saturdays for picnics. One time we went to our favorite place, which was an open grassy spot near the little train station that brought people to the spa. When we got there, our little hill was crowded with people. Festive. We didn't know *what-all* was going on. The station was decorated with swastika banners, red and black. We sat down and unwrapped our sandwiches. Just then a train came puffing up to the station. The car doors opened with great fanfare. I didn't understand German very well. All of a sudden Franz turns white. *Ach, Mein Gott*, he says. It's the *Führer!* Dear God, so it was. Out comes a little man dressed in brown. Surrounded by guards in black uniforms. He struts up the station steps and waves his arms and shouts at us, only fifty feet away. It was sunny. I could see his face quite clearly. Mustache and all. The people around us were ecstatic. Especially the women. I thought Franz was going to be sick. Hitler was terribly crude. But I must admit it *was* thrilling. Isn't that awful to say? If Franz had had a gun with him that day, poor sweet boy, he might have changed the course of history. The Führer harangued us for about fifteen minutes, then they all got back in the train cars, Hitler and his guards, and the train pulled out and that was that. My picnic with Adolf Hitler. And now here I am, forty years later in Buffalo City, eating turkey. Isn't life a wonder?"

Mockingbird, church bells, sun breaking through low clouds. Water Street the Parthenon Diner. Pancakes and coffee. Move equipment up line from Acomico. Handcar onto coal siding. Secure track switch. Call dispatcher. Camera set up. Number Seven Northbound Extra due Baker's crossing 11:05 A.M. Meet W. F. at Buddy's Lunch. Ask more about Springs. Check library. Industry past and present. Lime kilns. Iron. Site of ancient furnace. Quarries, lumbering orchards, mineral baths, tourism etc. Indian settlement. Graves. Confederate movements (Jackson?). Survey maps. Late dinner with A., Hotel Camden. Footpath through the darkened spa. Fireflies. Verandah hung with paper lanterns. Creaking stairs, an odor of cedar. Stripes of moonlight on the bed.

They must have named Acomico station after the residence. There is not much else up that way but fields and woods. My brother Wylie, when he was a boy scout, he camped out in those woods one time and he saw a bear. Just recently I read that some bears had been spotted along Powhatan Creek. Years ago, you have to imagine, that land must have been all cleared out for planting. I have a book (*Shades of Virginia*, Old Dominion Press, Richmond, 1956) where it mentions Acomico: "The last surviving heir was Ruhamah Garland, a widow. In 1875 she sold Acomico to Mr. Wolf" (aptly named), "who purchased the old house as an investment. Its fine paneled interiors of walnut and mahogany were removed. He sold the marble floors. Mantel by mantel, panel by panel, he stripped the interior bare of the work of the craftsmen who had lavished their care upon its embellishment. He removed 'the avenue of ancient and stately cedars' leading to the house, which were sawn up to make barrel staves. Even bricks from the graveyard wall and from the family tomb were sold . . ."

It still amazes me, the empty houses you see in Virginia, as if the families just suddenly decided to *leave* them. I've never seen anything like that up north. Old places, sometimes with furniture. Farmhouses. Even grand dwellings like Acomico. Anywhere else they'd be vandalized or burned down. And you can just go right in there. Hack through the brush, open the door and walk right in.

One mile north stands Acomico, bui in 1795 by Matthew Rosewell, nephe of Temple Clayborn, of Beau Fleuve The noble design of this house, with flanking dependencies, follows the p ciples of Palladian adaptation set fort in Robert Morris's influential book o 1757. Although a tradition of fieldsto construction had already been introduced to the Valley by Scots-Irish immigrants from Pennsylvania, the s brick masonry of Acomico, laid in Flemish bond with random glazed headers, reverts to the earlier English style of coastal Virginia. The interior avoiding baroque forms or elaborate plasterwork, demonstrated the tenac of late colonial tastes, with its fluted pilasters and wainscot paneling. Wh some materials were imported, the carved sills, quoins and splayed linte are all of locally quarried limestone. This superb example of late-bloomir Georgian architecture awaits an uncertain future, standing now derelict and all but hidden from view under Nature's green encroaching mantle.

Powhatan Valley
Architectural Survey, 1982.

II. Acomico

One mile north stands Acomico, built in 1795 by Samuel Rosewell, nephew of Temple Clayborn of Beau Fleuve. The noble design of his house, with its flanking dependencies, follows the principles of Palladian adaptation set forth in Robert Morris' influential book of 1757. Although a tradition of fieldstone construction had already been introduced to the Valley by Scots-Irish immigrants from Pennsylvania, the solid brick masonry of Acomico, laid in Flemish bond with random glazed headers, reverts to the earlier English style of coastal Virginia. The interior, in avoiding Baroque forms or elaborate plaster work, demonstrates the tenacity of late Colonial taste, with its fluted pilasters and whimsical panelling. While some materials were imported, the carved sills, quoins, and splayed lintels are all of locally-quarried limestone. This superb example of late-blooming Georgian architecture awaits an uncertain future, standing now derelict and half-hidden from view under Nature's green encroaching mantle.

Powhatan Valley Architectural Survey, 1992

It's hard to picture Anna walking along the railroad tracks with Russell, much less helping him or whatever she did. While Russell focused his camera on the "disordered beauty" of some grim little town like Ravine, it would be more like Anna to make pictures in her notebook of the clouds, or some trees, or a row of pigeons sitting on a wire. Not the darker realities. Russell's theory was that Anna's fierce determination kept her "perversely innocent." Her way of acting brisk and cheerful no matter what, like some actress in a French movie. Something formal and distant about her. Impenetrable.

I'd call Anna a compulsive decorator. Wherever she goes she always carries a little sketch pad in her purse or in her pocket. She would take it out and start drawing anywhere, in restaurants, at concerts, on a train, even at the movies. Pages and pages of ballet dancers, cows, waitresses, ice skaters, zoo animals, bicycles, flowers, sailboats, birds, fire hydrants, cellists, trucks, seashells . . . Those notebooks, she must have hundreds of them piled up on her shelves.

When Anna showed her work in New York in 1975, the art critic for the *New York Times* praised my sister for her "naive sensibility." Russell always maintained that Anna's whole knowledge of the world came from reading old *National Geographic* magazines. She knows all about Persia, Abyssinia, and Zanzibar. And my sister could chatter on forever about Matisse, or Fellini, or lemon pie, or the Marx Brothers, or zebras or *The Marriage of Figaro*. But try to get Anna to talk about something personal, or mention any topic like war or disease, and she would change the subject. I don't have time to be sad, she'd say. That used to drive Russell crazy. Talking to Anna, he said, is like trying to discuss philosophy with a cat. I could sympathize with him on that one.

Every named place on the line was be documented. I rode with Anna o motorized handcar borrowed from t section crew. There was barely roon aboard among all the heavy toolbox to set up our camera. On Sundays t ran no daylight trains; then we had t rails to ourselves. This track hadn't s passenger service for years. We work like thieves, stealing images, as train riders do, from that passing world unmasked by the railroad whose intrusion helped create it. A corridor c random and disordered beauty, the backs of buildings, a space where nothing is posed. You would walk h as a trespasser, stepping over weeds cracked pavement, past a rusty fenc chained dog, a string of white laund a man fixing his truck, a woman lyir in the sun . . .

POWHATAN
ARCHIVES
RAILROAD
M.F.

Every named place on the line was to be documented. I rode with Anna on a motorized handcar borrowed III. *Ravine* from the sectionmen. There was barely room aboard among all the heavy tool boxes to set up our camera. On Sundays they ran no daylight trains; we would have the rails to ourselves. There hadn't been any passenger service through here for years. We worked like thieves, stealing images. What we saw — from the train — was a world unmasked, a corridor of windows and disordered beauty, created and revealed by the railroad's intrusion. We steal its secrets from behind, where nothing is posed. Places where you would walk only as a trespasser, over weeds and cracked concrete, past a rusty fence, a chained dog, a string of white laundry, a man fixing his truck, a woman lying in the sun...

RAVINE

Chinaville is a mile off the Camden Springs road. I've never actually seen the town. The railroad built a branch line down there in 1940 to serve the glass sand quarry. Beyond Camden Springs, Powhatan Creek is called "Lost River." It flows north straight into Jupiter Ridge and disappears underground for two miles. It emerges in a deep gorge. The railroad would have extended its Camden Springs branch further south in 1875 if not for that obstacle. They wanted access to the timber. They finally laid a narrow-gauge line (two feet between rails) through the gorge in 1921 to meet the Powhatan at Camden Springs. And they did haul lumber out of there for a number of years. (This information comes mostly from Russell's notes.)

Construction of the Powhatan's Camden Springs branch (see map, p. 18) went so slowly that the financiers got impatient and decided to have a "golden spike" ceremony at Chinaville, even though six miles of track past that point had yet to be laid. So all the dignitaries gathered that day (June 14, 1874), and each banker, they had soft hands and they were full of whiskey, each took his turn swinging the maul to have a whack at the "last spike." It took ten men so long to knock in that one spike that the band had to repeat the final chorus of "Bless'd Be the Tie that Binds."

He'd been up there once or twice, and, like his father's hometown, it ha a flavor that was typical of the valley. One of his grandfather's dipsomaniac brothers lived there, a sly old bachelo named Vernon. This fact he happene to mention over coffee, to a woman I met at a lunch counter in downtown Baltimore. "Chinaville!" she exclaim softly. "I went there once. In June. I spring fever. I borrowed a car. I drove get lost, wherever the roads would lea It was exhilarating. Like falling, or floating. I finally stopped at a town. Chinaville. The name got me. I walk down every street. All those old build pre–Civil War, and not, you know, fi up. I wanted to melt into them. Two whole hours I sat on the front stoop o an apartment under someone's windo Breathing honeysuckle, listening to t wrens in the ivy. There was a TV goi inside, and a baby crying. The smell of greasy cooking, of poverty. No viev just a railroad embankment. What I f was perfect peace. Timelessness. Just being. So beautiful, so ordinary. I'll n forget it."

IV. Chinaville

He'd been up there once or twice, and, like his father's hometown, it had a flavor that was typical of the valley. One of his grandfather's dipsomaniac brothers lived there, a sly old bachelor named Virgil. This fact he happened to mention over coffee, to a woman he met at a lunch counter in downtown Baltimore, "Chinaville!" she exclaimed softly. "I went there once. In June. I had spring fever. I borrowed a car. I drove to get lost, wherever the road would lead. It was exhilarating. Like falling, or floating. I finally stopped at a town. Chinaville. The name got me. I walked down every street. All those buildings, pre-Civil War, and not, you know, fixed up. I wanted to melt into them. The whole town sat on the front steps of its apartment, under someone's window. Breathing honeysuckle, listening to the wrens in the ivy. There was a TV going inside. A baby crying. The smell of greasy cooking, of poverty. No view, just a railroad embankment. What I felt there was perfect peace... Timelessness. Just being. So beautiful, so ordinary. I'll never ..."

CHINAVILLE

Growing up around here in the late forties, it was hard to escape religion. Hymns and folklore. The camp-meeting Christianity of our grandparents' generation was full of Old Testament images. They entered our minds and we were not immune to them: The ground opened and it swallowed the sinner, and his wives *and his children* and all their animals. You're fed these images early and you're stuck with them for life. I have an idea (from things she said when we were kids) that Anna was haunted by, I don't know, biblical fears, her idea of hell, being separated and alone. In the end I think she went through *something*. And, if this doesn't sound too poetic, even if she came out strange, she came out whole.

What happened was in 1977 Anna got sick. Hospitalized for stomach trouble. But it wasn't only physical, I guess she was having some kind of breakdown. That whole dark time, it lasted a year or two, I rarely saw my sister. No one did. She was in Johns Hopkins for a while. She said not to visit, so I didn't. When she came home Russell took care of her. He proved reliable then. Even if he was (maybe) part of Anna's problem. It got to the point where if Anna was leaving the house, say, to walk the dog, she would *only* walk to the right, she just couldn't turn left, that sort of thing. Russell only told me later how bad it was. Anyway . . . Anna eventually got well. She went back to working harder than ever. She still had her enthusiasms, her artful ways and jolly quirks of mind. But she seemed changed. She seemed incredibly fragile and incredibly strong. (She didn't like to be hugged.) Later Russell told me *Anna is a great teacher.* He wasn't kidding. We were sitting at the bar at Abbott Brothers, in Shenandoah. I said, what does she understand that you don't? "Impermanence," Russell said.

Two miles west was located the camp meeting ground from which the present-day hamlet of Sunday Grove takes its name. The land was given by Virginius Dameron in 1817 to the Methodists of Appotomac County as place to hold services. In 1829 an open air auditorium was built, with beams hand-hewn from native pine. By the 1800s ornamented wooden cottages replaced the canvas tents of early day and thousands flocked to summer camp meetings from as far as Richmond or Baltimore, traveling by train or carria to hear the renowned orations of Dr. H. M. Weems. The site is presently occupied by the Beulah Abyssinian Baptist Church.

Road sign, state historical marker (unnumbered).

V. Sunday Grove

Two miles west was located the Camp Meeting Grounds from ... the present-day hamlet ... Sunday Grove derives its name. The land was given ... ginius Danforon in 1817 ... the Methodists of Appotomac County, as a place to hold se ... In 1829 an open-air auditorium was built with ... and hewn from native pine. By the late 180o's or ... al wooden cottage had replaced the canvas tents ... early days, and thousands flocked to summer camp m ... rom as far as Richmond or Baltimore, ... raveling by train or carriage to hear the renowned ord ... Dr. H. M. Weems. The site is presently ... occupied by the Beulah Abyssinian Baptist Church.

— Road Sign, State Historical Marker (Uncounted)

My grandfather Jerome Caton first met Norah Taliaferro (pronounced *Tolliver*) at a dance in 1898. The Pavilion Ball was held in Egypt every year around Christmastime at the old Temple Hotel. It was a fancy candlelit event, and they served holiday punch. Invitations went out all over the county. Egypt was harder to get to in those days. Most of the guests arrived by train and stayed over at the hotel. Grandpa was nineteen at the time. They say Norah was quite a beauty. She was only sixteen, but she fell for Jerome, and she fell hard. Jerome, well, he was already engaged, and he went ahead and married my grandmother, Wanda Levitzky. Then, two years later Norah was chosen Queen of Egypt at the Pavilion Ball. Jerome's younger brother Raleigh (Russell's grandfather) danced with Norah that fateful night. Raleigh fell in love with the Queen of the Nile. In 1903 Raleigh Caton and Norah Taliaferro got married.

Each brother had three children. World War I came along, and the great flu epidemic. Wanda and her daughter (Dad's sister Lucia) both died of influenza. At that time Grandpa was living up at Engle, West Virginia, near the old family quarry. Dad was eleven, and his father became a widower at forty. And here's where Norah Taliaferro Caton reenters the picture. I've seen the photographs of her. She was still good-looking at thirty-seven. One day, so the story goes, Norah pays a call on Grandpa to console him on his loss. I guess the "consolation" got a little out of hand. (This is the disputed part.) Then Raleigh, who was famously hotheaded, barges into his older brother's house and finds his wife there with Jerome. They say Norah was minus some articles of clothing. The next part no one disputes: Raleigh Caton smashes Grandpa in the face with a two-by-four. And that's how Grandpa came to be blind in one eye.

The amazing part is Raleigh and Norah stayed together after that, and they went on to raise up those three kids. One of them, Daisy, became Russell's mother. Grandpa Jerome was so well liked, his reputation didn't suffer at all. Jerome went on to marry an attractive young widow named Gladys McInturff. Miss Gladys had been Dad's grade school teacher, and Dad always maintained she would never have gone *near* Grandpa if the stories about him had been true. So Gladys became stepmother to Dad and his brother Stanley in 1921. Jerome and Raleigh lived on into the 1950s, but neither brother ever met or spoke to the other again. The offspring (our dad and Russell's mom) inherited the silence, and it mostly held firm, until Russell broke the ice with Anna.

There are no pyramids here, nor prie The local royalty, identified as *Phara* in gold script across their crimson var jackets, gather to smoke cigarettes an play pinball down by the underpass o Railroad Avenue at the New Nile Lounge. From this sanctuary it is onl short walk uphill to the town center, where a twenty-four-foot stone obelis rises above an island of greenery, surrounded by a traffic circle. Cars ar trucks detour around it as horse wago did before them, as if this mechanize form of ritual encirclement were a wa of maintaining veneration, though th monument itself may command only fading respect, or barest interest, from the descendants (including some pre day Pharaohs) of those slain young m of Egypt in whose memory it stands. inscription in the pale marble reads FALLEN IN BATTLE above a bronze plaque with the names of forty-three Confederate dead. Nearby, among th holly bushes, a mossy granite base ma the site of a companion statue, plann in 1879 but never built. Her shadowy image is preserved at the courthouse, the framed drawing of a weeping Nic entitled *Egypt Mourns Her Sons*—ar unknown.

Aurora Xenia Rivers.
"Towns Along the Powhatan Line."
Shenandoah 9 (May 1984): 17–25.

EGYPT

Russell's notes that I've been quoting from don't contain anything really personal. No clues. No revelations. A few pages are missing, though. Whether Russell or Anna removed them is anyone's guess. All these notes, as well as the map (p. 18), come from Russell's dog-eared railroad diary. Russell kept lists of railroad names. Sometimes he copied them from passing trains. You'll have some freight cars in a train, they'll be twenty and thirty years old,* or older, depending on what type of car it is, and they'll be lettered for railroads (Russell called them "fallen flags") that no longer exist. Some of these cars might be traveling a hundred or a thousand miles from home. Russell said the names of American railroads read like "automatic poetry":

Wabash, Monon, Cadiz, Katy, Erie, Seaboard, Cliffside, Frisco, Rutland, Rio Grande, Grand Trunk, Cotton Belt, Ann Arbor, Rock Island, Santa Fe, Arcade & Attica, Bangor & Aroostook, Belfast & Moosehead Lake, Rahway Valley, Unadilla Valley, Lehigh Valley, Sumpter Valley, Live Oak, Perry & Gulf, Gulf Mobile & Ohio, Baltimore & Ohio, Chesapeake & Ohio, Florida East Coast, Elgin Joliet & Eastern, Delaware Lackawanna & Western, Toledo Peoria & Western, Chicago & North Western, Green Bay & Western, Norfolk & Western, Western Maryland, Chicago Great Western, Great Northern, Apalachicola Northern, Northern Pacific, Union Pacific, Duluth, Winnipeg & Pacific, Butte, Anaconda & Pacific, Central Vermont, Central of Georgia, Jersey Central, Maine Central, New York Central, Illinois Central, Bonhomie & Hattiesburg Southern, Wyandotte Southern, Milwaukee Road, Nickel Plate Road, Burlington Route, Natchez Route, Detroit & Toledo Shore Line, Skaneateles Short Line, Atlantic Coast Line, Soo Lines, Reading Lines.

*As late as the 1950s, wood-sheathed boxcars and fifty-year-old hoppers were still plentiful on many U.S. railroads.

In the wonderment of its poverty-enforced dilapidation the Powhatan might seem to favor beauty over fun as if it were merely a linear museum contrived for the display of machine artifacts, a theater or temple in railro form consecrated to moments of tra side epiphany. The weed-grown right-of-way veers westward from B Junction at Damascus, climbing an winding through a narrow valley thi nine miles into the Appalachian foo Unscheduled freight movements ha by steam locomotives still provide th drama and the lifeblood of this back woods route. Four whistle blasts ech mournfully down the line, signaling train's approach to the Burma Road crossing. As coal smoke billows thro treetops, the massive engine heaves view. Driving wheels churn ponder under the reciprocal thrust of piston cranks and side rods, the visible me anism of external combustion, trust worthy, satisfying, mysterious and a inspiring. In the locomotive's sooty aftermath a trainload of hopper cars rumbles past with 1,000 tons of cru stone. The brakeman waves from th rear platform of his caboose as the t recedes noisily down the track, pass out of sight around a curve through gap in the swaying trees.

Odessa Cross. *Short-Line Survey.* Shenandoah: Indigo Press, 1962.

M.F.

POWHATAN   POWH...

PTN 67   PTN 69

VII. Wilderness

In the wilderment of its poverty-enforced dilapidation the Powhatan might seem to favor beauty over function, as if it were merely a linear museum conceived for the display of machine-age artifacts, a theater or temple in railroad form, consecrated to moments of trackside epiphany. The weedgrown right-of-way veers westward from the A. & S. junction at Damascus, climbing and winding through a narrow valley 39 miles into the Appalachian foothills. Unscheduled freight movements, handled by steam locomotives, still provide the drama and the lifeblood of this backwoods route. Four whistle blasts echo mournfully down the line, signaling a train's approach to the Burma Road grade crossing. As coal smoke billows through treetops, the massive engine heaves into view. Driving wheels churn ponderously under the reciprocal thrust of pistons, cranks and side rods, the visible mechanism of external combustion, trustworthy, satisfying, mysterious and awe-inspiring. In the locomotive's sooty aftermath a trainload of hopper cars rumbles past with 1000 tons of crushed stone. The brakeman waves from the rear platform of the caboose as the train recedes noisily down the track, passing out of sight around a curve, through a gap in the swaying trees.

— Cross, Odessa. *Short-Line Survey*. Shenandoah: Indigo Press, 1962.

I remember one time we were over at Anna's for dinner. Russell had been up to Powhatan, West Virginia, to the coal mine. Anna was trying out some Greek recipe. We had a big bottle of *ouzo*. Russell picked up a copy of *Artforum* magazine that Anna had lying around. "*Structuralism.* That's all we need, more brilliant ideas from France. Easy for them to 'demystify' what *other* people make since they don't *make* anything themselves. Now they say you can't trust photographs to tell the truth. Is that news? Since when did photographs ever tell the truth?" I forget what else Russell said, but he went on about Palmer & Hammond, the old-fashioned studio he worked for. How commercial studios used to paint and retouch prints, to "bend reality" to suit their clients. It was common practice. Using pictures to tell lies. I found this passage in Russell's notebook that comes from around the same time (June, mid-seventies) as the dinner at Anna's:

The workplace, in old photographs: sanitized and immaculate. Some studio artist would retouch the prints, paint out all the clutter. Factory grounds with no evidence of humanity or disorder. Nowhere the grimy buildings of real life: tile chimneys spouting black smoke (unrepentant). No skyline cluttered with water towers, utility poles, power lines. Greasy earth, weedy lots strewn with rotten lumber and old piles of scrap metal. Polluted ditches. Or the adjacent precincts: identical ranks of row houses in working-class neighborhoods, Irish, Polish or Negro, their saloons and betting parlors. Or behind them, the intricate crazy quilt of backyards, the ramshackle display of chicken coops, trash cans, clotheslines and vine-covered trellises. But how do you apply "aesthetics" to these sad and damaged places? (Agee's dilemma in Alabama.) How to do them justice? I say "beautiful" anyway, not knowing what other word to use. If I say "I am moved" by the beauty of that coal mine (whose workers are no doubt abused and underpaid) and by the crumbling and polluted landscape around it . . . What rules, what morals apply?

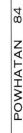

POWHATAN
ARCHIVES
RAILROAD

M. F.

COAL &

VIII. Powhatan

In 1904, after five years of arduous construction, a railroad was completed across the state line to reach the coal company's Powhatan mine, in Eaton County. The Powhatan Seam lies surrounded by shale, in an area of abundant limestone. It appears on geological survey maps as an island anomaly, a small pocket of semi-anthracite (86% fixed carbon) extending S.W. to N.E. approximately ten miles, in the Valley of Israel Creek. One must travel some 50 miles west to find the nearest neighboring coal bed. This lies in the Alleghany Formation, a low-volatile (78% to 86% fixed carbon) bituminous deposit known as Upper Rainbow...

Lawrence, Ursula R. "Strange Beauties: Nature and the Industrial Terrain." Virginia Geographic Quarterly 65 (Spring 1959): 72-86.

Here Anna and Russell are on their way to see Virgil Ross, the model-railroad genius. Russell talked about their visit for weeks afterwards. The night before, they had stayed in Egypt, at the old Temple Hotel where the famous ball used to be held. That much is clear. But Nehi is where things start to get murky. I know that road, but I could not find that house or any place like it. Mind you, Nehi is tiny. If the house burned, I didn't see a foundation. I keep recalling one of Anna's lines: *There's no such thing as a true story.*

Russell was so earnest about wanting to document and record these scenes, and getting the facts right, I've been taking my cues from him, always referring to *Stations* as "Russell's album." Not even Professor Stillwell could figure out how much Anna might have had a hand in reshaping it. My first good sit-down look at the album, when I realized what a chewed-up mess it was, I thought maybe it was some perverse trick of Anna's . . . her way to get back at Russell, to make his "great project" look like the dog's breakfast. Revenge. Because he floated around Anna for almost twenty years without ever committing himself (although I always figured that was part of the attraction), or because *nobody* could ever measure up to her dead brother Wylie, or because finally Russell didn't save her . . . from God knows what. That's one possible explanation. The other is that Anna's "intervention" (as Stillwell calls it) was her gift to Russell. Maybe, in spite of all the *feeling* that went into his photographs . . . maybe the original album was a little too, oh, factual, or pedantic (just like Russell was sometimes). It must have taken terrific devotion for Anna to do what I assume she did, rounding up the originals from God knows where, finding quotes for each picture, copying them and so forth. In this way you could argue that Anna breathed new life into the album.

We head south after breakfast, M. [Russell McKay] driving. Narrow roa[d] through the Powhatan Valley, hemm[ed] in by railroad tracks and the creek. A pilgrimage to visit R. [Virgil Ross], to see the basement empire of model tr[ains] for which, among fellow devotees, h[e's] become legendary. Strange obsessio[n] the spatial alchemy of miniature wor[lds]. Bewitchment. Subtext of unexamine[d] symbols. M., speaking their language comes and goes like a spy. The railro[ad], he says, is an archetype of all Paths. [We] drive past some small frame houses a[t] Nehi. M. looks over to the tracks. Ah[,] a slender brown woman appears on [a] porch. A sibyl. One arm raised, as if [to] warn or bless. As we pass, she gives u[s a] riveting look. (Toy memories, shiver[,] thrill, little blue watchman with the lantern, waiting for a train, to pop lik[e a] cuckoo out the door of his trackside shanty.) M. looks at me. That was so[me]thing, he says. Wasn't it?

Journal of Anna B. (c. 1978).
[Shenandoah Public Library]

ACTION AT NEHI

Here, on the afternoon of Septembe[r] 1864, Painter's cavalry, bypassing en[-] trenched Federal positions to the ea[st] surprised and captured a party of Un[ion] observers attempting to ford the mu[ddy] creek. The place became known as Knee-High Crossing, later called Ne[hi].

Road sign, state historical marker no. B-19.

NEHI

There haven't been any cougars in this area for over a century. Probably some early settler encountered a "panther" along here, and that's how the place got its name. The railroad must have had a hell of a time building that tunnel. They used hand drills and horse-drawn carts and they blasted out the rock with black powder. It took them eight months to go through five hundred feet of rock.* Railroads often followed river valleys (in this case, Powhatan Creek) to take advantage of the natural gradients, but building tunnels was not something they liked to do. Smaller railroads like the Powhatan didn't have lots of extra capital to spend on reengineering the landscape. It was hard enough just to lay in the ties and get the rails spiked down.

With *model* railroads, it's the opposite. The more tunnels the better. A perfect way for trains to appear and disappear. There's a certain thrill to that, as I learned. After his first visit with Virgil Ross (the model-train wizard) Russell went back again and he brought me along, to see the setup. Mr. Ross received us into his house and showed us down to the basement. The railroad spread out everywhere around us, but the scale was tiny. Lots of tunnels, of course. In one place he made a little valley, and I realized it was an exact duplication of the cut at Panther. Tunnel, track, rocks, even the foliage. A freight train ran through on its way to somewhere. Magical. It gave me a funny feeling. I never saw anything like it.

pan´ther, 1 pan´ther; 2 păn´ther, *n.*
1. A leopard from southern Asia, esp. one of black or dusky coloring. Symbc of worldly pleasure in Canto I of Dant *Inferno.* 2. Commonly, a large Americ carnivore, such as the puma (*Felis con color*), which ranges n. from Canada s to Patagonia; or, sometimes, the jagua of S. America. 3. **Pan´ther,** A town in McDowell Co., W. Virginia (pop. 60(on the Norfolk & Western Railway m; line. 4. An unincorporated village in Appotomac Co., Virginia (pop. 72) on the Powhatan Railroad line. (See Taliaferro, p. 143.)

Cochrane's Book of Knowledge. Baltimore: Bay Press, 1929.

*Odessa Cross. *History of the Powhatan Railroad.* New York: Parthenon, 1987.

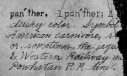

PANTHER

pan'ther, 1 pan'ther; 2... *pän'ther* ...of Worla... ...ch as the p... A leopard from southern Asia, esp on... lack or dusky color. Symbol... in line. 4 ...*felis concolor*), which ranges n. from... American carnivore, s... or, sometimes, the jagu... un A town in McDowell Co. W. Virg... & Western Railway m... (see also Talladega... corporated village in Appotomac... Powhatan R.R. line. ...n. 143)

X. Panther
Commonly, a large
...da s. to Patagonia;
...op. 600), on the Norfolk
...inia (pop. 72), on the

Cochrane's Book of...　　Baltimore: Bay Press, 1929.

PANTHER

I don't recall much about Virgil Ross, except that he was heavy and shy and he wore thick glasses. All that detail work must have strained his eyes. He began as a painting restorer and had a job with the National Gallery. He made some good investments and was able to quit work in his mid-thirties, with just enough income to live on. From then on he devoted himself full-time to his hobby, building scenery and laying track. His miniature railroad was largely based on the B & S (and the Powhatan), "with a large piece of Baltimore thrown in for good measure." He planned the whole landscape beforehand, with dozens of maps (track plans) that he drew to show the geography. Mountains, rivers, everything, down to the last detail. Russell said Anna behaved herself during their visit. I'm sure *he* could have stayed all day. When Anna got bored, she got out her pad and pen and started to sketch. Not the fabulous scenery, Russell said. No, Anna sat down and started drawing pictures of Virgil Ross! I guess Mr. Ross was a little nonplussed (not too comfortable around women), but in the end, Russell said, she charmed him. I wish I could see those drawings. But I remember: she gave them to Mr. Ross. They must have gone up in the fire. Here are some of Russell's thoughts (from the diary) after that visit:

RAILROAD: Metaphor? Freudian symbol? They [hobbyists] are driven by obsession, like me (but theirs is covert, unexamined). Some of us express longing through art, others in more private ways. Compared to artists, who are too self-aware (Anna, a wondrous exception), I find the devotion of these anonymous hobbyists often stranger, more profound, more moving. The intimate world of obsessed amateurs: outwardly ordinary but inwardly focused, like addiction, on some private creative pursuit. Model railroaders, tattoo artists, trout fishermen, stamp collectors etc.: Masters in their chosen realm. A man's world: Grail Quest in an enchanted forest of gizmos. Passion breeds its own subculture, its own heroes (Virgil Ross), its own literature and terminology, a whole vocabulary of shared mania.

Virgil Ross lived at 36 Arch Street, a modest house chosen for its "basemen potential." Here Ross worked for seven teen years to create his sprawling Lilliputian domain, the complex land scape of a fully operational railroad in miniature, "so realistic it was breathtaking," recalls a neighbor. Visitors to this cellar labyrinth entered, through narrow aisleways, a shoulder-high panorama of minutely detailed scener A network of tracks linked the rural terrain to an urban valley crowded wi model buildings, replicating the grim architecture of Ross's native Baltimore Ross, a shy bachelor with a flair for drama, would turn the power switch, illuminating at one stroke a twilight v of backyard America: factories, shops, row houses, trees, streets and bridges, and now and then a distant train rumbling off into some tunneled dark ness. For Ross it was easier to "talk sh than to try to explain his passion. "Th is theater," he once offered, "with trai as actors. The play is about arrival and departure. Like life. A mystery." Virgi Ross, 59, died on May 7 of heart failu On May 18, when the house on Arch Street was struck by lightning and burned, it was a sad and fateful epilog for the theater of trains.

"Artist with a One-Track Mind." *Powhata Gazette.* May 31, 1982.

"Rainbow Gap—
check town hall records
for architect's plans?

M. F.

BUFFALO & SHENANDOAH R.R. TRACK PLAN

XI. Rainbow Gap

Virgil Ross lived at 36 Arch Street, in a frame house chosen for its "basement potential". Here Ross worked for 17 years to create his sprawling Lilliputian domain, the complex living forge of a fully operational railroad, in miniature. "Perfect realism. It was breathtaking," recalls a neighbor. Visitors to this labyrinth entered a shoulder-high panorama of minutely detailed scenery. Trackwork linked the rural terrain with a complex urban valley, its grimy architecture modeled after Ross's native Baltimore. Mr. Ross, a shy bachelor with a flair for drama, would turn a switch, illuminating a twilight vista of backyard America: factories, shops, row houses, trees, streets and bridges, with now and then a distant train rumbling off into some tumbled darkness. For Ross, it was easier to talk shop than try to explain his passion. "This is theater," he once offered, "with trains as actors. The play is about arrival and departure. Like life. A mystery." Virgil Ross, 59, died May 7, of heart failure. On May 13, the house on Arch Street was struck by lightning and burned, a sad and fateful finale for the theater of trains.

"Artist with a One-Track Mind." Powhatan Gazette, May 31, 1982.

RAINBOW GAP

Great-Aunt Odessa had seven brothers and no sisters. She took Grandpa's side in that mess between the two brothers. After the "Norah business" she always referred to Russell's grandfather as *that thug Raleigh*. I don't reckon she had much use for men anyway. Her early marriage to "Mr. Cross" was mysterious and brief. That was Odessa's place, up there in Vermilion. In later years she shared it with another of the brothers, Oscar, and he had his own separate house on the property, what used to be an old garage. Odessa lived by herself in the main house. I remember her coal-burning Kalamazoo kitchen range ("Kalamazoo Direct to You"). Cream color and green. Odessa shoveled coal and chopped wood until the day she died, age eighty-seven. She kept an iron tea kettle steaming on that stove. Russell said if you want to learn something about steam locomotives, just learn how to operate Odessa's stove. I don't know where Anna got her hands on that letter from W. J. to Russell, but it must be real (she could never have made up "Vauclain compound" or "Walschaert valve gear"). I do know W. J. used to go up there sometimes to look in on Oscar, his wife's uncle.

Odessa Caton wrote a number of books and articles about the history of this area. I used to be scared of her. She didn't much like little boys. Right up until 1970, when her eyesight began to fail, she'd be driving all up and down the county in that old dark blue DeSoto of hers. She bought it new in 1940. I can still see her, she'd have on a man's workshirt over some old print dress, and there'd be a Lucky Strike stuck to her lower lip. Dad would never ride with her. Once I asked him why not (I think I *knew* why not). Because she drives English style, he said. What do you mean? I asked him. What I mean, son, is she drives *on the wrong side of the road.*

Dear Sonny,

Just a quick note from your old man.
Visiting Uncle Oscar, up in Vermilio
Same old game, he keeps his whiske
hidden behind *The Book of Knowled*
I play along. You'll be glad to know t
Powhatan is still steam powered. Wh
a marvel. Remember how you used t
run to Oscar's porch to watch? An ol
ten-wheeler was switching boxcars th
morning at the feed mill. She came
from the B & O in 1953. The braken
told me. B & O class B-18c, a 1901 A
built Vauclain compound, converted
simple, with Walschaert valve gear. T
whole language, too, passing away. O
has TV now. The news is about rock
ships, but here I look out the screen
on a scene from decades past. Coal t
in the valley. Hell of a lot of smoke.
Smudge of time across the sky. Stead
billowing of past and present . . . the
constantly amazing overlap where w
are. Tomorrow I'm taking the train to
Egypt.

As always,
Dad

Letter, August 5, 1960.

Dear Sonny,

Just a quick note from your old man. Visiting Uncle Oscar, up in Vermilion. The old games, I play along. He keeps his whiskey hidden behind The Book of Knowledge. You'll be glad to know the Powhatan line is still steam powered. What a marvel. Remember how you used to run to Oscar's porch, to watch? At the feed mill this morning, a ten-wheeler was switching freight cars. She came from the B&O, in 1953. The brakeman told me. It's a class B-18, a 1901 Alco-built Vauclain compound type, converted to simple with Walschaert valve gear. The whole bridge trembled as she passed. Oscar has T.V. now. The news is all about rocket ships, but here, I looked out the screen, saw, in a scene from decades past. Coal train in the valley. Hell of a lot of smoke. Smudge of time across the sky. Steady following of past and present, the constantly amazing overlap, where we are.
Tomorrow, I'm taking the train to Egypt.   As always—Dad

M.F.

XII. Vermilion

— Letter, Aug 5, 1960

VERMILION

This story (from one of Russell's letters?) about the Sunday drives, if it was published, Anna must have sent it to her editor friend in Baltimore, after Russell's death. *Or did she just make it up?* I was visiting her one time, Anna had this beautiful big studio room at her old place in River City, and Russell was there and she was showing us some of her new work. It was late. Anna went to the kitchen to make coffee. The parrot was sitting on Russell's shoulder. Russell stood there in the lamplight and looked at me and he said *Anna has no scruples.* I realized he was praising her. He criticized himself for being *too* scrupulous. He envied Anna's freedom to borrow and invent whatever suited her purposes. Her art wasn't bound to a subject, he said, in the narrow way that his was. And Anna could admit all kinds of flaws and imperfections into her work. She was always improvising. She just made up whatever she needed to. That night I remember she showed us this amazing painting, it was more of a construction actually, it had leaves and figures running through it, and in one place there were some dark round holes in it and I said, what do these dark holes do? and she said *they hold dark air.*

NOTE: B & S Junction, on the Powhatan line, is in fact the same *place* as Damascus (see map, p. 18) on the B & S. Similarly, the next and final stop is downtown Shenandoah, but it is designated *City Station* on the Powhatan timetable. In order to reach the city, Powhatan trains, by means of a "trackage rights" agreement, actually travel on B & S rails for a few miles. Thus two stations here have dual identities, as they are served by both railroads. Russell McKay apparently decided to make the most of this situation by adding an extra picture for each of these two "overlapping" station stops.

Sunday mornings we'd go for a drive down the Valley Road, with me in the back seat and the radio tuned to "The Symphony Hour." We crossed the B & S tracks at Damascus, right by the junction where the Powhatan line comes in. You could see the other rail curving through the truss bridge across Euphrates Creek. Uncle Vernon would point, "Look, Sonny: there's the way to Egypt." And it was true, Egypt was up the line, about sixteen miles, near West Virginia. The city I envisioned had sphinxes and palm trees in it. Of course this picture got corrected eventually, although the junction, when we would pass it, seemed as compelling as ever. It beckoned like a gateway to some other landscape . . . who knows what. But anywhere the currents of travel intersect is a charged place. Start there, say, and you can feel the presence of other localities, known or imagined, far down the line. But we are always "here," never "there." And that's the paradox. It's as if we savor that dislocation, even as it prompts our desire for seamless unity. What we have, what we inhabit, is a geography of longing.

"Eyewitnesses." *Baltimore Journal of Industrial Archaeology* 11 (1983): 15.

XIII. B & S Junction (Damascus)

Sunday mornings we'd go for a drive, down the Valley Road, with me in the back seat and the radio tuned to the Symphony Hour. We crossed the B & S tracks at Damascus, right by the junction where the Piedmont line comes in. You could see the other rails, curving through the brass bridge across Euphrates Creek. Uncle Vernon would point, "Look, Sonny: there's the way to Egypt." And it was true. Egypt was up the line, about 15 miles, near West Virginia. The city I envisioned had splinters and palm trees as well. Of course that picture got corrected by reality. But the junction, when we would pass it, seemed as unsettling as ever. It hinted, like a gateway to some other landscape, who knows what: it implies here the currents of travel intersect in this actual place. Start there, says, and you can feel the presence of other localities, known or imagined, far down the line. But we are always 'here' never 'there'. An irresistible paradox? ?, as if we savor our dislocation, as it prompts our desire for seamless unity. What we have, what we inhabit, is a geography of longing.

"Eyewitness", Baltimore Journal of Industrial Archeology, Vol. III, p.15.

B & S JUNCTION - DAMASCUS

Passenger business on the Powhatan was almost dead by the late 1950s. The only regular riders left were the maids who lived in Shenandoah and commuted up to Camden Springs to work in the hotels. Service was down to once a day, round-trip. People clamored to be on that last train. Russell took Anna along, and she wrote me about it (I was away at school). They rode to Camden Springs and back. The engine, number 12, was retired five years later, but it was saved by some railroad enthusiasts. A dozen volunteers worked eight years to restore that old steam locomotive. Here is Anna's letter:

dear lucky,   *River City, Oct. 7, 1960:*

I hope i hope you like the faulkner book i sent. When you finish, then i will start you on Proust. Please allow two years. And please (since you do so well in French) explain to me why they translate "Temps Perdu" as "Things Past." Why not "In Search of Time Lost"? "Past" is not the same as "lost"! You'll see Proust is full of music, and yes I miss music, to answer yr question. A big ache. I have dreams about playing and my heart remembers but my fingers have forgotten and last nite I dreamed Ignatz Mauser was standing by the piano dressed in a tuxedo and I was performing the mozart C-minor fantasy, only i kept missing notes, and i looked up and he turned into a large mouse, he was sitting on the piano and he was crying, and i said i'm sorry, i'm sorry, and i was crying too and then i woke up. I cannot pursue both things. I'm painting day and night. In class and at home. I have mozart and schubert to listen to on the hi-fi and they are my friends and they keep me company (such company!) when i work. Russell took me on a train ride last week, the last train to egypt, it had a steam engine, to R.'s delight. It was rather sweet and poignant except oscar caton was on the train, soused, and he gave me the cold shoulder. I tried to be nice, for R.'s sake. He says i should vote *(for kennedy), and so i will. Now i'm working on some new pictures: birds, different colors, different repeated shapes in a grid, and I think they are much better than the dancing figures you saw before. R. is threatening to buy me a parrot.*

Love, A.

At 5:30 P.M. on September 30, 1960 Egypt westbound train no. 7 pulled Shenandoah Station and steamed u Pluto Street bridge on the first leg of its final 29.1-mile trip to Cam Springs, thus bringing to a close mo than half a century of passenger ser on the Powhatan Railroad. The trai consisting of locomotive no. 12 follo by a baggage car, mail car and two green coaches, rolled south on rails the B & S along 1.3 miles of shared before diverging at Damascus Junct onto the Powhatan's own line to beg its run up the valley through Vermil Nehi, Egypt, Sunday Grove and Camden Springs. Only a few tracks onlookers were present to mark the occasion. Among the passengers abo for this twilight excursion, the moo was bittersweet. Local historian Osc Caton summed up the feelings of m "I came to bid farewell to a piece of history, a familiar landscape, a whol way of life . . ."

"Last Train to Egypt."
Powhatan Gazette. October 1, 1960.

XIV. City Station (Shenandoah)

On September 30, 1960, Egypt westbound train No. 1 pulled out of
City Station and steamed under Pluto Street bridge on the first leg of its final 29.1 mile trip to Camden Springs,
bringing to a close more than half a century of passenger service on the Powhatan RR. The train, consisting of
engine No. 12 followed by a baggage car, mail car, and two dark green coaches, rolled south on rails of the B & S along
the old track, before diverging at Damascus Junction onto the Powhatan's own line to begin its run up
through Vermilion, Nehi, Egypt, Sunday Grove and Camden Springs. Only a few trackside onlookers were present
for the occasion. Among the passengers aboard for this twilight excursion the mood was bittersweet. Local historian Oscar Caton
summed up the feelings of many: "I came to bid farewell to a piece of history, a familiar landscape, a whole way of life..."

"Last Train to Egypt," Powhatan Gazette, Oct. 1, 1960.

CITY STATION-SHENANDOAH

SMOKE

After the book fair, driving home on Route 11 from Marveltown, it was still sunny, late afternoon now, but dark gray thunderclouds were gathering in the north up the valley where I was headed. That would be good, the fruit trees needed rain. I had that package with the album in it beside me on the seat of the truck. No chance to really look at it yet. Almost like having a passenger sitting there. I was still seeing Sophia Garland in my mind's eye, and all those books laid out, and the Athenaeum and the sunlight and shadows around it. Memories came up . . . things that hadn't crossed my mind for a long time. Russell. Twenty years ago. A vision of Anna and Russell together, when they used to come over in the summertime, dusty and windblown after a day's photographing and riding in that little yellow motorized track car out on some godforsaken branch line of the railroad, and we'd all sit around on the back porch, in those green golden evenings, when I was still learning how to be a farmer. The lawn sprinkler would be on, with a rainbow in it, and Suzanne would make tomato sandwiches fresh from the garden and we'd pass around a jug of cider, cool from the springhouse, and the cicadas would be throbbing like waves in every tree, and Jake Miner would chug by on the tractor and wave, my trusted helper, younger than me, the kindest man I ever met, who could and did fix nearly every piece of equipment on the farm that ever broke, which at one time or another was just about all of them, who was still trying to pull himself together out of alcoholism after Vietnam, and we would all give Jake a wave, and would go back to talking again, and after a while the sound of a train would come drifting up through the orchards, the muffled distant throb of diesel engines, the steady soft rumble of the train, the diesel horn sounding its warning at the Farm Road grade crossing, *waaaaunnh waaaaunnh wauh waaaaunnh,* and Anna would say to Russell, not like the old steam whistles, eh, Mac? just to get him going, and he would, of course, he always did, about how diesels had no soul, how the steam locomotives were like living things (didn't we all remember?) because they breathed, because they combined all the natural elements, you know, of earth (coal) and water and fire and air, and how they moved, how you could see that churning movement all displayed, the great flapping of rods and the rolling of giant wheels, and on and on, until maybe Suzanne or someone would pretend to argue with him and say, but Russell what about the smoke, that terrible black coal smoke, and the pollution? and Russell would continue and explain how a good engineer always kept his smoke white, how black smoke was the sign of poor combustion, how railroads even used to plant inspectors along certain routes to take note of the smoke, and in some cases engineers who were careless in this regard could be fined, and how nowadays the tourist trains were creating a terrible image and a false impression by "hamming it up" with as much black smoke as possible, just to please the so-called rail fans, and by now Russell would be in high gear, standing and waving his arms about, and then he would sort of wake up, as if from a dream, and see that we were having fun with him, even Anna, or maybe especially Anna, because she loved this crazy wound-up part of him, and he would stop suddenly, red in the face and sheepish, or else he would yell at us some more, how we were just blind or not sensitive, not to care as much about these things, not to see their importance, as much as he did, and how it was not true that he, Russell, was hopelessly mired in The Past, because after all The Past was Everything, even twenty minutes ago was The Past, when we were finishing up our sandwiches, gone now, as surely gone as the world of the steam locomotive, which ended for most of the country in 1957, the same year his great-uncle Vernon bought a brand-new tail-finned pink Cadillac Sedan DeVille, and so what was the difference then, Russell would demand, between twenty minutes and twenty years? we didn't even know the meaning of nostalgia, tossing that word around like an accusation, it's from the Greek word for grief, *nostos* and *algos,* "past" plus "pain," don't you see? Russell going on, but tiring now, defused by Anna's smile, not really angry, and soon, slowing, we would all lapse into quieter talk as the sky began to darken, feeling the breeze start to rise from the west, as it always did and still does on this hilltop when there is any breeze at all to be had, then we would drift, deeper into that soft stillness, pleasantly, with only a word or two spoken now and then, and finally none, none being necessary, and we would sit quietly rocking in the porch chairs, drinking the last of the cider, listening to the wind come up and the crickets starting their songs, and the stars would begin to come out one by one, as the sky began fading from burnt pink in the west into blue black above, the night settling down gently upon the house, enveloping first the distant hills, and then the orchards, and finally the barn, and the trailer next to it where Jake lived, the tractor parked there now, and the pump house, and the clotheslines, and the rustling broad-branched oak tree, hiding all, filling the spaces between us with sweet silent darkness . . .

ACKNOWLEDGMENTS

Stations began as thirty-eight paintings and ended up as a book. Inventing a text to accompany the pictures proved to be more complicated than I had imagined. I would like to thank my friends, and everyone who encouraged me throughout the difficulties (and pleasures) of this project.

Thanks to Jacqueline Onassis, whose heartfelt enthusiasm gave me the confidence to go forward, and who understood what this book wanted to be even before I did. And to Larry Shainberg, who patiently read, corrected and cheered my shaky steps towards authorhood. Thanks also to Sharon Cooke and Andra Samelson for their readings and their comments. I am especially grateful to Dan Frank, whose fine skills as an editor have shaped and clarified this text in ways that I could never have done. And thanks to Fearn Cutler for her elegant design.

Thanks to Penny Pilkington and Wendy Olsoff of P•P•O•W Gallery in New York; to Trinkett Clarke of the Chrysler Museum in Norfolk, Virginia; and to Barbara Fendrick and Christopher Sweet, who helped the *Stations* paintings to be seen.

To Margo Herr, gratitude beyond measure for her valuable criticism, for bearing with me throughout, and above all for her love.

ABOUT THE AUTHOR

Michael Flanagan was born in 1943 and grew up in Baltimore, Maryland. He moved to Ohio at the age of eight, where for several years he lived in a house overlooking the tracks of the Baltimore & Ohio Railroad. He studied painting and photography at Parsons School of Design, worked briefly as a laborer on the Richmond, Fredericksburg & Potomac Railroad, and then attended Yale University School of Art and Architecture. Since his first solo show in New York, in 1981, his paintings and drawings have been exhibited in museums and galleries here and abroad. He has received a New York Foundation for the Arts fellowship in painting, and two grants from the National Foundation for the Arts. Flanagan lives in New York City with his wife, the artist Margo Herr. This is his first book.